Playing

like a Girl

Transforming Our Lives Through Team Sports

Marian Betancourt

Contemporary Books

Chicago   New York   San Francisco   Lisbon   London   Madrid   Mexico City
Milan   New Delhi   San Juan   Seoul   Singapore   Sydney   Toronto

Library of Congress Cataloging-in-Publication Data

Betancourt, Marian.
    Playing like a girl : transforming our lives through team sports / Marian
Betancourt.
       p.   cm.
    ISBN 0-8092-9812-0
    1. Team sports for women—Social aspects.   2. Team games—Social
aspects.   I. Title.

GV709.B48   2001
796'.082—dc21   00-48610

Contemporary Books

A Division of The McGraw·Hill Companies

Copyright Acknowledgments
Excerpt from "Girls Just Want To Have Fun" by Robert Hazard. Copyright © 1979
Sony/ATV Tunes LLC. All rights administered by Sony/ATV Music Publishing,
8 Music Square West, Nashville, TN 37203. All Rights Reserved. Used by
Permission.
Excerpt from *In These Girls Hope Is a Muscle* by Madeleine Blaise. Copyright ©
1996. Grove/Atlantic, Inc. Used by Permission.
Excerpt from *The Girls of Summer: The U.S. Women's Soccer Team and How It
Changed the World* by Jere Longman. Copyright © 2000. HarperCollins Publishers.
Used by Permission.

   2 3 4 5 6 7 8 9 0   VBA/VBA   0 9 8 7 6 5 4 3 2 1

ISBN 0-8092-9812-0

This book was set in Minion
Printed and bound by Maple Vail

Interior design by Monica Baziuk

McGraw-Hill books are available at special quantity discounts to use as premiums and
sales promotions, or for use in corporate training programs. For more information,
please write to the Director of Special Sales, Professional Publishing, McGraw-Hill,
Two Penn Plaza, New York, NY 10121-2298. Or contact your local bookstore.

This book is printed on acid-free paper.

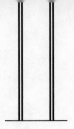

For my granddaughters, Hilary and Julia, free to be athletes

~

"That's all they really want
Some fun
When the working day is done
Girls—they want to have fun
Oh, girls just want to have fun."

—PERFORMED BY CYNDI LAUPER

~

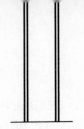

CONTENTS

PART II ∿ SEXUAL POLITICS:
MEN VS. WOMEN WITH BALLS

PART III ∿ TRANSFORMING OUR LIVES

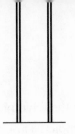

FOREWORD

I AM EXCITED TO HAVE the opportunity to support a book project that embodies so much of what I have dedicated my life to being a part of—a team. We are a part of so many teams throughout our lives: in school we work on academic teams to complete projects and assignments, at home we are part of a team that helps each other out and takes care of one another, and at work we team up to meet the objectives of the company and further the mission of the organization.

Playing like a Girl: Transforming Our Lives Through Team Sports is an inspirational and educational analysis of sports as a forum for women to come together as a team to reap all the benefits that sport has to offer.

The rise of women's sports in the United States and the world has been huge. It was particularly evident at the 2000 Olympic Games in Sydney, Australia, when the Olympic community celebrated 100 years of women in the Olympics. The cultural impact of this opportunity for women to perform on a world stage before billions of television viewers cannot be overestimated. These women, and all women who participate in sports, help support the dreams of all girls, reinforce public support for gender equity, and challenge the limitations that still exist.

As women in sports continue to achieve, they help to eliminate myths and stereotypes that spread beliefs that women lack the physical ability and mental fortitude to excel and compete under pressure in sports and other human pursuits.

I figured out early on that I wanted to be part of a team and I knew that sports were the team for me. Two of the happiest events of my life were being named to the U.S. National Women's Basketball Team and playing in the 1976 Olympic Games. I was only 17 years old, but it seemed like I had waited forever to be a part of something so great. From my days of playing pick-up basketball at courts throughout New York City, I had a goal and a dream that came true when I was named to the Olympic team. Being a part of that team gave me a sense of pride and happiness that I had never felt before.

My career has been one of firsts and one of great accomplishments. I was the youngest basketball player in Olympic history to win a medal when I helped the U.S. Olympic Women's Basketball Team win a silver medal at the 1976 Games. I had the honor of being a part of two Olympic basketball teams, and I was the first woman ever to play in a men's professional league. These and other highlights of my career are so important to me because they have shaped me into the well-rounded person and team player that I am today.

I didn't want to play in a men's professional league. I wished that there were a women's professional league that I could play in. But I loved the game, so I decided to be part of a men's team. I wasn't playing for money and I wasn't playing for notoriety. I was playing for all the right reasons—because it was in my heart. That is why the creation of the WNBA was such an important success for women's sports.

For me, the start of the WNBA made me think how grateful I am to have had someone like Billie Jean King, who put herself on the line 25 or 30 years ago. She was doing what young girls and women are doing today in sports before it was popular. Billie Jean never played basketball, but her fingerprints are on the WNBA. Her fingerprints are on women's professional softball, soccer, golf, tennis, and just about any other sport you can think of. She risked her reputation and her career because she believed so strongly that women should have the right to play on and to be a part of a team. She knew then what so many people are just starting to realize now, and that is why she founded the Women's Sports Foundation. She believed that if we all work together, as a team, we can work out the difficult problems and enable all future young people, men and women, to be the best they can be.

The Women's Sports Foundation continues to work toward realizing Billie Jean's dream. The Foundation works to give girls and women the opportunity to fully experience and enjoy sports and fitness with no barriers to their participation. I am so proud to be the president of an organization that not only provides opportunities for girls and women in sport, but also was started by a woman who I so greatly admire.

I hope women and girls everywhere will read *Playing like a Girl* to see how the joy of playing team sports can change their lives. I especially encourage women who think it is too late for them to begin, and those who think their participation in team sports must end after high school or college. Team sports are now lifetime sports for women.

—Nancy Lieberman-Cline

ACKNOWLEDGMENTS

THIS BOOK COULD NOT have been written without the enthusiasm and cooperation of all the women you will meet in these pages. There are far too many to name here, but some gave much more than I expected, and for their generous spirits, insights, and efforts, I'd like to thank these women (and this man):

Mavis Albin of Livingston, Louisiana, for her devoted and speedy attention to my constant digging for information.

Kathleen Connolly of New York City, for unselfishly giving up her lunch hour.

Elizabeth McCarthy for her time and introductions to others as well as for her very thoughtful responses to my questions.

Virginia Amos of Alexandria, Virginia, for finding me a hotel room on a sold-out night.

Mary McNichol of Wayne, Pennsylvania, for driving me back on the coldest night of the winter after playing a winning game of soccer.

Marcy Bright and Jen Stitzell for their over-the-top enthusiasm for ice hockey and for helping me bring that to the book.

Diane Hein for getting other softball players interested in telling their stories.

Filmmaker Gina Prince-Bythewood of Los Angeles, California, for her honesty and candor.

Bill and Pat Kennedy and their daughter, Kelly, of Barrington, Illinois, for sharing so much of their emotion.

Dr. Jo Hannafin, founder and codirector of the Women's Sports Medicine Center at the Hospital for Special Surgery in New York, for her thoughtful insights into women and sports.

Carole Oglesby, Ph.D., head of WomenSport International, for sharing so many personal insights and feelings.

Joy McCarthy, Ph.D., for remembering to get back to me, even while stranded at an airport.

There are many, many more who were helpful to the completion of this book, including Marj Snyder and Kristen E. Conte at the Women's Sports Foundation, Kim Soenen of Chicago, and Katherine Wheeler, attorney, of Baton Rouge.

I'd also like to thank my agent, Vicky Bijur, and my editor, Judith McCarthy, for their enthusiasm and support.

INTRODUCTION

I BELIEVE THE GROWING participation of women in team sports is the single most important development in helping us achieve self-esteem, equality, and power. The camaraderie and pride of this shared effort and experience also fill a soulful need. This is why team sports are more important than solo sports like golf or tennis, which tend to be elite. The team is a community that any woman can join. And millions of women of all ages are pioneering this new frontier.

What will develop in this new century? Will we be stronger and braver? Will we have better jobs and better pay? Will our daughters follow in our footsteps? Will our sons learn a new way to relate to women? How will our relationships with men change now that we can share something they always owned? This is a provocative topic, and with this book I want to ask the questions that will make you think about what is going on. I am not a social historian, a professor of women's studies, or a sportswriter. I am a student of the human condition, and this book is a look at what I see around me. I see that women are changing the face of all sports, too—the way all athletes are coached. I see that we are changing how corporate America looks at women. And I see a new breed of role models I wish I had when I was growing up.

Actually, this book began a long time ago, when I was 12 and scorned by boys and girls alike for wanting to play basketball. A boy on whom I had a raging crush told me to "act like a girl" when I accidentally hit him with a basketball. His contempt devastated me, and I skulked home to sit on the stoop, determined to learn how to be a girl, no matter how depressed that made me. I no longer remember that boy, but what he said remained one of those powerful freeze-frame moments of universal loss, like the death of Elvis. Something was denied to me at a time when I was full of energy and dreams. At that time, I had no clue that I could do anything about it. There were no girls' teams in the public schools, no hint of women athletes in the newspapers, on the radio or TV, in the toy stores, not anywhere. Although I did not realize it at the time, my early turnoff to sports was universal. Many women in this book got the same message—and still get it—that girls are not supposed to play team sports.

I know now what that early loss cost me and many other women who never played team sports. We did not learn about physical confidence and trusting our bodies. We did not learn how being part of a team teaches you not to take things personally in the "game" of business. Nor did we learn how being tall means you should see yourself as a leader—the way tall men do—rather than a misfit. And we did not learn that having an honest outlet for aggression means a woman would not have to use indirect aggression, primarily aimed at other women, in the competition for a man. Over the years I didn't follow team sports much. If I couldn't play, why get all excited about watching men play? It would only make me resentful. Jealous. I became like so many of my peers whose eyes glaze over at the mention of sports. It's a guy thing.

However, I did support and encourage my son and daughter to participate. My son was recruited heavily by colleges for basketball, and I was so impressed with the intensity and competition among recruiters and the outrageous tactics involved that I wrote a candid story for *Sports Illustrated* about what the experience did to the entire family. I remember asking one coach whether they were giving scholarships to women yet (Title IX had already passed), and he looked startled.

"Why?" he asked. "Do you want to play basketball?" At the time we were standing in the gym of my son's high school and the girls' team was warming up. The obvious was lost on him. My daughter also played basketball in high school, but she and others on her team were not recruited with the same zeal as the boys. In fact, the half-dozen schools that showed interest were so lackluster in their efforts that we hardly remember the experience.

But as women's team sports became a reality, the glaze over my eyes lifted. I began to identify and cheer. The first time I went to Madison Square Garden to watch a WNBA Liberty game, the roar of the fans when the team walked onto the floor in the packed house knocked me out. And I was not alone. More than 10,000 others seemed to have the same reaction.

Now, two generations later, I have two granddaughters who love to play team sports. Hilary, ten, and her younger sister Julia, eight, have been playing team sports since they could walk, and Hilary has already announced that she'd like to play in the WNBA (Women's National Basketball Association). I've seen her dribble the basketball behind her back, I've seen her shoot from the corner, and I have watched how she focuses when she plays, truly a member of a team. I have no doubt she will accomplish her goal. I've watched Julia move a soccer ball around the field as if it were a natural extension of her foot. And when she walks up to the plate in a baseball game, she whacks the plate hard, swings the bat up to her shoulder ready to tear the cover off the ball, and makes a gritty face at the pitcher.

One evening during the final phase of writing this book, my son called "just to brag." Hilary had just struck out the opposing team's batters in two innings of her kids' baseball league. On the field, she got three runners out on grounders. She's the only girl on this team because the leagues in that suburb are organized into baseball or girls' softball. Both my granddaughters chose baseball. In the entire league there are 80 boys and 5 girls.

One of my best memories is playing "imaginary" baseball with Hilary and Julia one morning before leaving their suburban home to return to New York. I pretended to be the radio announcer, calling out the shots while they pitched, swung, and ran bases—without a ball or bat or gloves—as the sun filtered through the trees on the bright, green summer morning. I love this! Finally, I can live out my own lost yearning.

Playing like a Girl is meant to inspire and inform not only those women already involved in team sports but the growing numbers of women who are looking for teams to join. It's for parents of daughters who love to play team sports, and for daughters who want to encourage their mothers and grandmothers to play team sports. And it's for fathers who have found a new way to bond with their daughters and who have become some of the most devoted fans. (Yes, men have been liberated, too.)

What do these teaming-up women have in common? They have fun—and this is their primary reason for playing team sports. They also share many other benefits, such as improved self-esteem and confidence, feelings of strength and power, and greater satisfaction in their work and social lives.

What impressed me most in talking with women of all ages and from all over the country was the fierce passion and commitment they feel about playing on their teams, whether it's ice hockey or basketball, soccer or rowing. These women represent millions of others around the country who are doing the same thing, some for the first time in their lives. I've always been a sucker for stories of determination and for those who overcome the odds to do what they want—women who fell down many times before they were able to walk (or skate); women who, often for the first time, understood the sense of belonging, the adrenaline rush of physical competition, and the shared camaraderie that comes from riding home on a bus with the rest of the team after a good game. Men have known about these things for a long time. Now it is our turn.

I hope you'll read *Playing like a Girl* as an inspiration as well as a guide to participation. There's a comprehensive resource section to get you started looking for a game or finding teams and leagues around the country.

While my granddaughters have no clue that they are the least bit unusual because they love—and can play—team sports, there is still a very strong mind-set about who can be an athlete. When a new six-year-old boy joined Julia's class at school in 1999, he assumed she was a boy because she was good at sports. When this newcomer told his father about his new friend "Julia" who was a boy, the father asked him if Julia wasn't a girl. The boy said, "No, he can't be a girl because he's good at sports." Once this kind of assumption is no longer made, we will have truly arrived.

I wanted to write this book not only to exorcise that ancient insult from a boy in my youth, but for women who got similar rejection, and most especially for my granddaughters and their peers who are entering a new millennium of equality in sports.

Those memorable moments that turned us away from sports in childhood have been replaced with new ones: Karyn Bye's face on front pages around the world as she waved the flag after the victory of the United States Women's Hockey Team at the 1998 Olympics, Brandi Chastain whipping off her shirt—whatever your opinion about that!—at the World Cup soccer championship in 1999, the New York Liberty's Teresa Weatherspoon making that miraculous winning shot from across the court at the buzzer in the 1999 WNBA play-offs. Moments of pure joy.

I've waited all my life to write this book. I hope you enjoy it.

PART I

The Joy of Teaming Up

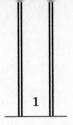

GETTING INTO THE GAME

~

"This is changing the landscape of America."

—Tipper Gore speaking on TV about a WNBA All-Star Game and the Women's World Cup soccer championship, July 14, 1999

Four million dollars. That's what gamblers plunked down on the 1999–2000 NCAA final basketball game between the University of Connecticut and the University of Tennessee. That was the most legal bets ever made on a women's sporting event according to *Sports Illustrated for Women* magazine. What could be more telling about how women's team sports have captured the American mainstream imagination? Unless it's the recent and first Nintendo video game featuring a female team athlete, Mia Hamm, who is now as popular among teens of both sexes as Michael Jordan, according to recent consumer polls.

The pundits who said nobody would pay to watch women play sports certainly have plenty of egg on their face since record crowds attend women's basketball and soccer games. The attention to

Women's World Cup soccer was not a surprise to anyone following the trend of growing audiences at professional WNBA games and women's college games. Television executives are falling over each other to buy into the phenomenon of so many millions of people watching women run and jump and sweat and knock each other down on TV. Women's college athletic programs are booming, and new women's professional leagues are blooming.

Women now account for 37 percent of college athletes, and in the 2000 Olympic Games in Sydney, Australia, 44 percent of the competing athletes were women. In 1996 and 1998 U.S. Olympic women's teams brought home the gold for hockey, basketball, softball, and soccer.

More than 90,000 people filled a Palo Alto, California, stadium on July 10, 1999, for the Women's World Cup in soccer. Another 4 million were tuned in to the television coverage and 500 reporters covered the game. In contrast, a broadcast on the same day of a men's baseball game in Philadelphia showed empty stands.

Nearly 2 million fans attended WNBA games in 1999, with average attendance around 10,000 and higher for games between combative rivals like the New York Liberty and the Houston Comets, which draw nearly 20,000 fans and are sold out as soon as they are announced. It took the men of the NBA 28 years to get 10,000 fans to a game. The WNBA did it in two. Television viewers were up to 50 million in 1999, 1 million more than the previous year. WNBA president Val Ackerman announced in 2000 that 2.5 million viewers a week are tuned in to the WNBA on NBC, ESPN, or Lifetime Television for Women.

Attendance at women's college basketball games tripled from 1984 to a high of 5.2 million in 1996. The women's college basketball finals had three times the Nielsen rating of men's hockey at the same broadcast time in 1999 and 14 percent better ratings than NBC men's professional basketball games (not to mention an increase in the number of gamblers, for whom there isn't a reliable rating system).

The success of the Women's National Soccer Team has also prompted colleges and universities to put up more money for women's soccer. Some call it the Title IX equivalent to football and now see women's soccer as a revenue-producing sport. The crowd for a midweek women's soccer match in 2000 at the University of North Carolina was nearly 5,000, up from just over 3,000 the previous year.

In fact, the National Collegiate Athletic Association (NCAA) appears to be doing some reverse discrimination by increasing the number of Division I soccer tournaments for women to 48 and holding the number of men's tournaments at 32. Women's programs have been given priority over the men's for the past few years. There are now 260 women's programs and fewer than 200 for men. Coaches in women's soccer programs are now under pressure to produce on the field, and this has resulted in higher job turnover.

When it comes to money, women now spend more on sports apparel and athletic shoes than men do. Women have outpurchased men in these categories since 1991, according to the Sporting Goods Manufacturing Association. Footwear is an $18 billion industry, and Nike, with its focus on women's sports in the "Just Do It" media campaign, has 37 percent of the market.

THE NEW GLADIATORS

The best news is that the rest of us—in droves—are getting in on the action. Team sports are no longer just for girls and women in college or professional leagues. Soccer moms are becoming soccer players. Women from all walks of life are teaming up for basketball, softball and baseball, volleyball, ice hockey, lacrosse, field hockey, sailing, rowing, and even football. They are secretaries and social workers, doctors and lawyers, police officers and teachers, systems analysts and stay-at-home moms. Most are in their 20s through 50s, and there are an increasing number of women over 60. These new gladiators play on community recreational leagues, with private sports clubs, and on semiprofessional and Olympic teams. Some women have never played team sports before, some are playing after years of abstinence following high school or college. Whatever the experience, women's team sports are the fastest growing sports in the country.

Several things are happening here. Government intervention has created more opportunity, public attitudes about women are changing, and corporations are putting money into women's sports. In the 27 years since Title IX changed the law to grant equal opportunity—and dollars—to women's sports, one in three girls, compared to one in twenty-seven, participate in sports, and these girls are more apt than are nonathletes to succeed in all areas of life.

- More than 7 million American women play soccer.

- Girls and women account for one of the fastest growing segments of USA Hockey membership categories with a 171 percent increase in women 20 or older. During the 1990–91 season, 5,573 female ice hockey players registered with USA Hockey. Now there are more than four times that many with more than 27,000 registered girls and women playing ice hockey in the United States.

- The Women's National Adult Baseball Association in San Diego reports 85 teams in 20 cities in America.

- More than 14 million Americans play softball, and half of them are women.

- Women's master rowing is the fastest growing women's sport, and women's crew had the fourth highest increase in participation among all NCAA sports in 1997.

- Volleyball, now an Olympic and professional sport, is dominated by women.

- More women and girls participate in basketball than any other sport according to the National Association for Women in Education.

- Women's lacrosse is growing by leaps and bounds. More than 20 schools were added to the list of colleges offering women's lacrosse in the first few months of 2000. High school teams grew from 562 to more than 1,000.

- The first all-women America's Cup crew inspired the phenomenal growth of women's sailing teams.

THE MOST AGGRESSIVE SPORTS ARE GAINING FASTEST

The latest Title IX report from R. Vivian Acosta and Linda Jean Carpenter, two retired physical education professors from Brooklyn College who have been keeping track of the progress of Title IX for more than a decade, tells us that most women are going after the more aggressive sports. The popularity of ice hockey is illustrated by the women in the next chapter, and the fledgling National Women's Hockey League is lining up media and corporate support.

Football

Football, perhaps the last bastion of male identity and domination, is being tackled by women, too. In its first year, 1999, the new Women's Professional Football League (WPFL), based in Edina, Minnesota, toured the United States with two teams playing exhibition games in Chicago, Green Bay, St. Paul, Minneapolis, New York, and Miami, and an exhibition at the Super Bowl in Atlanta in early 2000. By 2001 the league had 11 teams with more expected. Women's tackle football has been popular in Australia for 13 years, and the sport thrives in Germany and Tokyo, as well.

According to WPFL president Carter Turner, this is "real smash-mouth football." A 40-year-old woman who grew up playing football with her brothers told a *San Francisco Examiner* reporter that she had always wanted to put on the pads and play real tackle football. As a player in the WPFL, she gets to do this every Saturday afternoon. WPFL players have been quoted widely about how they love to crush their opponents, talk trash, and run opponents down. They have also said they like to get all that aggression out and then dress up and go out to party.

Players are paid $100 a game for ten games in a season that runs from October to February, so most have not given up their day jobs yet. In Colorado, 300 hopefuls turned out for tryouts for the Valkyries. Players come from the ranks of other sports and flag football, but many have never played football before. Some former NFL players are getting involved as coaches or owners, and coaches have also been recruited from high school and college teams.

Turner told a reporter at ABC News he was raised by feminists and is raising his own 16-year-old daughter. He believes the other half of America should be playing football.

Lacrosse

A field sport that began as a war game among Native American men, lacrosse is exploding as one of the fastest growing women's team sports, according to Cathy Samaras, who founded Quickstix with her husband so that their daughters would have a chance to play. (One of those daughters is now the assistant lacrosse coach at Yale University.)

"It's like lightning," Samaras said. "Kids go around and introduce it to others." More and more women are joining recreational leagues as well.

Samaras, 57, played lacrosse in college at the University of Maryland at Towson, but she quit because the game just wasn't fun if she couldn't play on a competitive team. There was no interest in women's sports, and, Samaras said, "It was more fun to go to my husband's school and party." Today the University of Maryland is the most competitive, with six national championships in women's lacrosse, the longest streak of national championships in Division I women's athletics.

Lacrosse is different from field hockey in many ways but most obviously because it makes use of a netted stick to scoop the ball off the ground and throw it. The stick is used to carry the ball down the field, catch the ball, and get the ball into the goal. The game is named for the French word for "the cross" because of the curved stick. Agility and speed count more in this game than do brawn and size.

The women's game, which began in Philadelphia in 1939, has no body contact, just finesse, Samaras said. Sticks can make contact, and some checking with sticks is allowed. Samaras said the goalie wears a helmet and the other players carry a stick and wear a mouth guard. Ironically, the lacrosse game women play today is more like the Native American game of the past than is the men's version.

According to Samaras, for the past 10 years Quickstix has been promoting the game across the country and getting it into the national spotlight. Quickstix trains coaches and umpires, administers leagues to increase opportunities for competition, and sends athletes to neighboring states and overseas. They sponsor a recruiting tournament for rising high school seniors where the players can be seen by more than 150 college coaches. Only 15 percent of the women's lacrosse coaches are men because, Samaras said, they don't know the game as well as women do.

One of Samaras's pet peeves is that "we have to call it women's lacrosse. When men play it is simply lacrosse."

Sailboat Racing

Sailboat racing is another highly aggressive team sport that has drawn women, especially since the 1994 America's Cup all-women team nearly won the race. Some women have raced with mixed-sex crews, but all-female racing teams now compete in tournaments like the competitive Rolex International Women's Keelboat Championship (RIWKC), which began in 1985 in Newport, Rhode Island. The event, held biannually, is sponsored by U.S. Sailing and was designed to encourage women sailors who want the challenge of planning, training, and competing together on keelboats.

The competition's original mission was to get more women into keelboat racing, according to Denise MacGillivray of Middletown, Rhode Island, chair of U.S. Sailing's International Women's Keelboat Championship committee. "Now women all around the world are organizing keelboat campaigns, and the event is well established as one of the highest profile, most competitive all-women keelboat regattas in the world," MacGillivray said.

In 1993 there were 43 teams competing, and that number increased with each event. When these women were asked what makes them rearrange their lives for this week-long trial, they said they love the competition—the physical, emotional, and spiritual challenge. One said, "It made me realize how fun the sport is and how much I still need to learn."

In 2001 the race was to be held in Annapolis, Maryland. The original J24 sailboat has been replaced with J22s, thus reducing team size from six to four and hopefully allowing more women to compete.

Womanship, a sailing school based in Annapolis, and *Sail* magazine surveyed 950 women in 1996 and reported that 87 percent claimed the best part of learning to sail was learning to be part of a team; 91 percent also cited the camaraderie.

The National Women's Sailing Association sponsors the aptly named "Take the Helm" program to teach women all over the country how to take charge at sea. They also sponsor AdventureSail for inner-city kids, a program that reaches more and more girls each year.

GOING PRO

With the success of Women's World Cup soccer and the WNBA, more professional sports leagues are being organized for women. In 2000 investors in the Women's United Soccer Association (WUSA) were reportedly putting up 5 million dollars each to launch at least 8 teams and to expand to 12 to 15 teams in cities such as Atlanta, Boston, New York, Detroit, Philadelphia, San Diego, Tampa/Orlando, and Washington, D.C. WUSA is a semipro league that operates under the umbrella of United Soccer Leagues (USL). Current and former college players, amateurs, and professionals make up the 36 teams in the United States and Canada. Members of the women's national team that won the World Cup have played in the USL.

Media companies, including Discovery Communications and AOL Time Warner, have committed $40 million to WUSA for the first five years and are projecting an average attendance of 6,500 with plans to present the games in 15,000- to 20,000-seat stadiums. Tony DiCicco, former coach of the United States Women's National Team, is the acting president of WUSA. Unlike the professional women's basketball league, which plays in the summer after the men's season ends, the WUSA playing season will coincide with the men's season from April through August. However, without the backing of an established organization like the NBA, WUSA may have more of a struggle getting started than did women's basketball.

Women's professional basketball has expanded faster than expected with the WNBA adding 4 more expansion teams in 2000, bringing the number of teams in the league to 16. In order to open a franchise, each team must receive deposits on 5,500 season tickets, and apparently this is not a problem. The original plan was to add two teams per year. Because of stable attendance and television ratings, as well as talent available after the demise of the short-lived American Basketball League (ABL), the WNBA added four new teams in 2000—the Indiana Fever, Miami Sol, Portland Fire, and Seattle Storm. (The first 12 teams were in New York, Houston, Orlando, Cleveland, Charlotte, Phoenix, Washington, D.C., Los Angeles, Sacramento, Detroit, Utah, and Minnesota.)

With the growing number of women athletes in college, there is a growing talent pool for professional leagues. Before the WNBA and the ABL, talented athletes who wanted to work had to join professional basketball teams in Europe. Now, girls and women coming up through the ranks are getting scholarships and being scouted and recruited to play at home.

Volleyball has the first professional women's sports league without a "W" in its name. United States Professional Volleyball (USPV) was organized in 1999. It is a professional volleyball league. Period. It is the first time in history a women's league will precede a men's league. USPV, six-on-six indoor volleyball, plans to expand in five-year increments with teams in the southeast, northeast, and west. It was scheduled to begin in January 2002 with 6 to 10 teams in Midwest cities and a season from January to April with finals in May. In the spring of 2000, USPV held the Millennium Cup with a $60,000 purse, the largest ever for women's volleyball. The televised event matched the American teams with teams from Japan and Poland. Arie Selinger, coach of three Olympic teams including the 1984 silver medal winners, coaches this new "Dream Team."

USPV has the backing of the Federation Internationale de Volleyball and USA Volleyball, endorsements that have helped organizer Bill Kennedy get the corporate backing the league needs. Interestingly, one of the USPV sponsors is Royal Neighbors of America, an insurance company that understands gender discrimination; it was founded in 1895 by a group of visionary women who wanted to offer insurance benefits to Americans through women and their families. Their mission, they say, is to protect the quality of life of women, their families, and those they care about. Royal Neighbors is providing 3 million dollars to USPV over four years. Ballgirl Athletic; *Real Sports*, a women's sports magazine; and several other businesses are also sponsors.

Kennedy, who wears bolo ties and a Stetson, is founder and CEO of The Kennedy Group of Companies, builders of customized single-family homes in the Chicago area. He likes to call himself "a builder of dreams." Perhaps the USPV Dream Team is the ultimate dream. He had strong motivation for organizing the USPV because he wanted to find a place for his tall and talented daughter, Kelly. It was only after he enrolled Kelly in a local volleyball program that she developed the self-confidence that turned her into an All-American at the University of Wisconsin.

His good fortune in business did not make Kennedy forget what was important to him. He said that in the early 1990s when there was talk of a professional volleyball league, he wanted to make it a women's league. Other potential investors disagreed, so Kennedy thought, "Well, OK, we'll do that later." However, the men's league didn't get off the ground, and in 1998 Kennedy made a commitment to sponsor a women's Dream Team. He wanted it to be something like the Harlem Globetrotters, a team he would take around for exhibition games.

Kennedy said starting the USPV was one of the hardest things he ever did, and he admitted it may not develop as fast as he'd like.

Two-time Olympic champs, the U.S. Softball team has inspired the beginnings of the Women's Pro Softball League (WPSL) with four squads in Ohio and Florida. Organized in 1997, the league seems a natural outgrowth of the International Women's Professional Softball Association, founded in 1976, which survived only four seasons. The new league has television coverage on ESPN and has recruited players from the Olympic teams of 1996 and 2000 as well as colleges.

FUELING THE GLOBAL ECONOMY

Not only are women playing and spending, we are becoming a behind-the-scenes force in sports, a $60 billion industry in the United States. Sports are bigger than the auto, petroleum, lumber, and air transportation sectors of the economy, according to the Women's Sports Foundation. Amateur and professional sports generate enormous amounts of money. Billions of dollars are spent for television coverage, product licensing, advertising, and endorsements.

Even though the sports industry is still predominantly male, and subtle forms of discrimination remain, most of the overt barriers are down. Corporations realize that there is a very lucrative market for women's sporting goods. The sporting goods manufacturing industry, which was until recently 95 percent male, formerly produced little or nothing for women. Women were also virtually nonexistent in the sports media, where all copy and air time was about men's sports. Marketing was male—men selling sports and men's products to men and male corporations. People now believe that their daughters can play sports and become anything they wish. These parents, the baby boomers, are holding the purse strings.

GAMBLING ON WOMEN

In the 21st century women are on our way, breaking new ground, but we still have a long way to go. Title IX may have changed our law to guarantee equal access to sports, but the social awareness still moves like molasses in some areas. Why else in 1996 would a high school girls' coach lose her job when she demanded equal facilities for the girls and equal pay for coaching? Why are mostly men still the coaches? And why would the Chicago Parks Department deny women their ice time for hockey? Why do stores still put sports equipment and games in the boys' section? And the big question: when will we be paid as well as men for the same work on the field or in the stadium?

These questions are explored in the following chapters. But most of the stories are about the happy warriors who finally are having their days on the fields, their dreams fulfilled in what were formerly "men only" arenas of sports and life.

The joy of playing with a team was mirrored in a TV commercial that had a short but memorable shelf life a few years ago. Women are in the street playing stickball with great gusto and noise. Suddenly, a boy calls out from a nearby stoop, "Mom, come on in. Supper's ready." His mother, busy running the bases, breathlessly replies that she cannot stop now. Then the boy tells her what's for dinner (the sponsor's product), and of course, she stops the game and goes home.

We have come a long way. We still have a long way to go, but more and more of the world is betting on women's team sports to achieve the stature and success of men's sports.

It's just a matter of time.

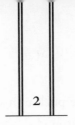

SOULS ON ICE

~

"The sports with the most sustained growth were the 'sweaty, grunty and aggressive' sports. That tells me that there is a sense of self-confidence among women today. They can participate in sports that bring them joy and society doesn't insist that they can't show aggressiveness or assertiveness."

—LINDA JEAN CARPENTER, *NEW YORK TIMES*, MAY 2000

THERE ARE FIVE MINUTES to go in a crucial play-off game. Chicago Ice defense player Jen Stitzell is feeling the pressure as she battles for position, trying to lift her opponent's stick with her own and intercept the shot without screening her goalie. Another opponent skates around the outside of the face-off circle, looking for the puck. Stitzell skates on it, and the puck deflects behind her. She panics for a second, unable to see the puck.

"Behind you, Jen," her goalie yells, and Stitzell whirls around, sees the puck, and shoots it to the opposite corner, where a quick teammate picks it up and passes it out of the zone. Whew! Stitzell relaxes for a second to catch her breath and then skates to position just inside the blue line and yells "Point!" for the puck because she is now open. Her opponent moves to cover her just as an Ice teammate passes the puck. The Ice has the lead with time winding down.

The opponents rush the puck up two on one. Stitzell's defense partner has gotten turned around so she stays in the middle, trying to play the pass. Reaching out one-handed, Stitzell barely gets the tip of her stick on the puck, but it bounces away before her opponent can get a shot off. The buzzer sounds. Stitzell raises her stick in the air and skates for the goalie to give her a bear hug as the rest of the squad, faces flushed and beaming, push up their masks, slap hands, and whoop it up. The Ice is going to the finals!

"Then it's time for the game-after handshake," Stitzell says, "where we tell the other team, 'good game,' and try to conceal our excitement so as not to rub it in. But the second we're in the locker room, it's celebration time. It's one of the best parts of winning a game, talking about it in the locker room right afterward."

The championship game is not until evening, so the women of the Chicago Ice have plenty of time to shower and have a group lunch in anticipation of the "big game" that night. Spirits are high, and the pizza tastes wonderful. Then, it's back to the rink for the final game where it starts all over again.

THE CURRENT STATE OF WOMEN'S HOCKEY

The explosion in women's hockey since the National Team's Olympic victory in 1998 has made some people forget that women have been playing this game for more than 100 years, just in smaller numbers. Isobel Preston, daughter of Lord Stanley Preston of Stanley Cup fame, was playing hockey on a flooded lawn in the winter of 1890. This is the earliest known image on film of women involved in a game of ice hockey. According to USA Hockey, there is little doubt that women played the sport well before the first newspaper accounts of a game between two unnamed women's teams appeared in the *Ottawa Citizen* on February 11, 1891. That game, which was played in Ontario, is now regarded as the start of women's ice hockey.

Today girls and women account for one of the fastest growing segments of USA Hockey membership. In the 1990–91 season, shortly before Mary Gutowski organized the Chicago Ice, 5,573 female ice hockey players were registered with USA Hockey. Since then, that number has increased more than four times with more than 27,000 registered girls and women playing ice hockey in the United States. In 1990 there were 149 girls and women's teams, and by 1998 there were 1,071.

Women's hockey is especially big in the Midwest. The number of girls' teams in the Minnesota State High School Athletic Association has zoomed to 112, up from 24 teams five years ago. In 1994 Minnesota declared women's ice hockey a varsity sport on the high school level. On the college level, seven Midwestern teams mushroomed at the end of the 20th century, prompting the Western Collegiate Hockey Association to create an official women's league.

Since the U.S. Women's National Ice Hockey Team won the Olympic gold in 1998, some sporting goods sales reps say they can't even give away figure skates. Girls want to be like Cammi Granato, captain of the medal-winning team. And the creation of pro teams is not far behind. In September 1999, the National Women's Hockey League (NWHL) made its debut in nine cities and towns across Canada. Though its players won't be paid, the NWHL is lining up corporate sponsors and courting the media.

THE WOMEN OF THE CHICAGO ICE

Jen Stitzell never forgot the way the guys laughed at the women hockey players in college, "as we walked across the campus carrying our hockey bags. They said it was sacrilegious for women to play hockey." Now on the intermediate B squad of the Chicago Ice, the 28-year-old CPA from Park Ridge, Illinois, said, "I never ever thought growing up that I would someday be standing near center ice getting ready for a face-off with a real official and real opponents. I love to play this game more than anything."

Stitzell and 50 other women from the Chicago area have come a long way since 1992 when Mary Gutowski and six women organized the Chicago Ice. In just a few short years, this adult women's recreational organization became a force to be reckoned with, and it has changed the lives of most of the women on the team. There are now three levels of expertise on A, B, and C squads, and the Chicago Ice competes in state and regional tournaments and is sixth in the Women's Central District League (WCDL) standings of USA Hockey. They sponsor their own annual tournament and have a website. Some members have tried out for the Olympics.

Marcy Bright, 32, is so addicted to it, she has learned to ignore her mother's pleas to stop playing around and get married. Laura Moss, 41, like many other women on the Chicago Ice, decided her kids didn't have to have all the fun. Carrie Matczynski, 28, never skated until she was 22, and Deb Siegel, a 44-year-old social work manager and mom, is making up for a lost childhood dream that was dashed when she was told as a kid that she could not play hockey because it was unladylike.

When Mary Gutowski was a sophomore at the University of Illinois at Champaign, she ran into a journalist friend in the laundry room one day who was doing a story on hockey and invited Gutowski to tag along to a practice session. She borrowed a pair of skates, and that was her first attempt at ice hockey. She played at college for two years and got a taste of competition at the tournaments, including Brampton in Ontario, which is the largest of its kind for women's ice hockey.

"A lot of men had a problem with women playing hockey," Gutowski said. "And they sucked," she added. "I have just as much right to play." Gutowski and a few friends joined a men's league, and because there were no facilities for women, they were forced to change into the 40 pounds of bulky hockey padding and bracing in the women's room of the ice arena. Gutowski asked the men if they would mind if she sat on the benches outside the doorway of their locker room to gear up. It takes as long as 15 minutes to strap on all the protective gear and suit up. Hockey players wear regular clothes under the gear, so her request was not exactly scandalous.

"They didn't know what to say," Gutowski recalled.

But playing on men's teams was not what Gutowski had in mind. She figured she and her friends could all do better, so after graduating from the University of Illinois in 1992, it was time to organize women. She had her own apartment, her first job as sales and marketing rep for a food company, and plenty of energy and free time.

"About five or six of us went to Denny's and sat around," Gutowski said. "Our goalie, a graphic artist, designed the logo after we picked the name. We chose Chicago Ice over Black Widows. A woman who was interested but could not make the late-night games donated $200," so the women got their team jerseys. Gutowski spent most of the time recruiting on the phone and putting up flyers in ice rinks. "This was before E-mail," she said.

Gutowski, who has earned the team nickname "the Goon," had been to Brampton, in Canada, and other big tournaments in the Midwest. "This opened my eyes," she said, and she wanted the Chicago Ice to compete on that level, too. "We were scrambling for bodies," she said, "so we had players with experience as well as novices." It was also hard to find coaches because there was no way to pay them.

The first Chicago Ice team had seven or eight players and no coach, but they scheduled their first tournament anyway and began making arrangements to play. Ice time is not easy to get because it is usually booked for a year in advance. Nevertheless, they found some available ice and booked it. The team scheduled a game, and the opposing team drove all the way down from Madison, Wisconsin. Once they arrived at the rink, the Chicago Park District told them, "Oh, sorry, your ice went to another [men's] team."

"They gave us drink tickets," Gutowski said, "so we took them to court. They had oversold the ice." Soon after, the Chicago Ice got a judicial statement saying they could use the ice.

Many girls grew up playing hockey on boys' teams, and, according to USA Hockey, half of all females playing hockey regularly play on men's teams. Chicago Ice's Laura "the Enforcer" Moss, for example, still occasionally plays on the men's team. But in general, girls and women are lost in the shuffle when they play with men. Women play a different style of hockey and can do this best with female teams. What women may lack in brute strength and limitations on body checking, they make up for in toughness and endurance. Checking is using a hip or shoulder to slow or stop an opponent who has control of the puck. Direct and intentional checking results in a penalty. The no-check rule for women allows players to concentrate on the skills of hockey—skating, passing, stick handling, and shooting.

As children, Moss and her brother watched every Chicago Blackhawks game on TV and skated every day on the ice rink just beyond their backyard. Nevertheless, Moss was discouraged by her mom who said, "You can't do this. You'll get hurt. You're getting breasts." Moss's only rebellion at the time was to use racing skates rather than the figure skates her parents insisted on. However, once she graduated high school her parents capitulated and bought her hockey skates.

Although she had been a hockey fan since childhood, it wasn't until she brought her own 3-year-old daughter to a kids' league that she began to play herself at the age of 35. "I wanted to make sure she had the opportunity I didn't have." Ironically, her daughter, now 10, and her 8-year-old son are soccer players with no interest in hockey.

Moss signed up for one of the ice hockey clinics for beginners and persevered. At first she played with a men's team, mostly because they were the people in her hockey clinic, and they all played together; she did not experience the harassment other women encountered. "It's because they weren't very good," she laughed. "You get pushed around a lot," she said, but that's the nature of the game. She described getting pushed around by a guy who is six feet four and weighs 240 pounds. Moss is no midget, at five feet seven and 140 pounds, but she said men have an advantage because they can skate faster. "But they're not smarter." Moss now plays on the Chicago Ice's A squad and is their treasurer.

Deb "Beave" Siegel, of Wilmette, Illinois, also had brothers and got to the Chicago Ice indirectly through boys' hockey. Both parents discouraged her from playing sports as a child because it was unladylike. But having two brothers, she did play with them. "I could run faster, throw better, and was always chosen over the boys and the girls in the neighborhood when we played pick-up games—football or baseball." She did play sports in high school, "but in those days there were no coaches, leagues, or uniforms."

Siegel is on the B squad and is in her fifth season with the Chicago Ice. "I was goaded into trying out because a friend of mine, who had a son on my son's hockey team at the time, wanted to play and didn't want to go it alone. I had recently started using hockey skates rather than figure skates due to a bunion on my foot. My son wanted me to attend a player/parent game on the ice, and I was unable to wear the figure skates. He insisted I try hockey skates as they [used only for men] are wider. I did. I could finally skate again! My friend and I took some adult beginning hockey classes then joined the team."

Her son, in seventh grade, plays ice hockey year-round and in-season baseball and lacrosse. "Playing sports has affected the family in many positive ways. We attend each other's games, and we have lots in common!" Siegel has coached her daughter in basketball and softball and her son in baseball, soccer, ice hockey, and basketball. Her daughter is a junior in high school and plays lacrosse.

About her own playing Siegel said, fear of injury "absolutely inhibits my game because I had knee surgery when I was in high school, and it's never been the same. I really have no business playing softball and hockey given the fragile state of my knees. I wear knee braces on both knees as a precaution, and I try not to take risks when I play." At one time, she said, "I injured my knee fighting for the puck in the crease [the demarcation line in front of the goal] and missed four weeks of playing."

Even with the risk of injury, Siegel said, "I enjoy that I feel like I belong there, on the ice or on the field. It is tremendously empowering. I love to use my body. The exercise is a major rush. Working as a team toward a common goal is the best. I have made this one of the priorities of my life because I always wanted to do this and never had the chance. I feel like I'm making up for lost time, and as long as I am able, I will continue to do it!

"I've always had a pretty kick-ass attitude," Siegel said, "but since finally being able to realize what's basically a dream I've always had, it has accentuated that attitude."

Siegel is also very involved in the administrative aspects of the Chicago Ice organization. She has served on the executive committee for four years and is the organization's secretary. She has produced the Chicago Ice program and tournament books over the years. Siegel said, "my coworkers are in awe of my passion for and commitment to hockey."

Passion and commitment are keys to the success of the Ice because the women spend a considerable amount of their own money and a huge allotment of time from their busy schedules for practice, games, and travel to an increasing number of tournaments. The Chicago Ice competes with five or six teams in a long season of 26 games from September through the end of April.

Equipment can cost $1,000 new or maybe $200 or $300 used. Skates alone are $300 to $400. Each team pays about $400 to be in the organization. Then there are fees for ice time at $125 to $225 per hour, and that is for one or two games every weekend.

"We do two types of fund-raising," Moss said, "general team funds and then stuff and money for our annual tournament. The general fund-raising takes the form of ads in our program book, and that's all cash. Mostly, people rely on personal relationships to raise that money. The team gives each player a 25 percent credit on all cash raised. For the tournament we ask for goods and money. Hockey companies usually supply us with a fair amount of goodies for giving away. We get cash again from the program book, and also this year Subaru sponsored us."

After seven years, Gutowski is surprised that it's still hard to get sponsors. "I thought it would be easy after the Olympic victory." While some local vendors donate equipment, it's difficult to get money, but in 2000 the team began to find more support.

Treasurer Moss said, "I'm not sure, but if I had to guess, I'd say it's harder [to raise money for women's teams]. I'm not sure most men's teams raise money. I think most of them just have their players pay a team due. Most men play in a house league, and the fees are usually lower. Here, every team has a different level of dues depending on where they are able to get an ice slot, how many slots the team has, and how many players [there are] to divide it over, less the fund-raising. Typically, our team has lower dues than any other because we have so many people to spread the costs over. We use our practice ice very efficiently—two squads splitting the ice for practice all the time."

Players must run their lives efficiently, too. Carrie Matczynski, a business development manager from Hawthorn Woods, Illinois, manages a competitive job with a competitive sport. While temporarily assigned to work in corporate headquarters in Indiana, she was driving five hours each way on weekends to get to hockey games in Chicago. She did this for three months and never missed a game. She also never had a weekend off.

Matczynski had never been on skates until she was 22. There was an indoor rink at the University of Illinois, where she was a student. It was there she learned how to skate. Since joining the Ice, Matczynski has worked her way up from the C to B squad. A is the most competitive level.

Matczynski is only five feet two and has what she describes as "a tree stump physique," yet her team nickname is "Graceful." She's among the shortest of the Ice players and often gets knocked down, so she works on balance. She broke her leg in a game against Wisconsin but said she didn't even know it was broken and continued to play. Then she was out eight or nine months until it healed. She has also hurt her shoulder. The team has no medic, but another player who is a trainer for a high school team does what she can to keep the team healthy.

Matczynski said she is more aggressive and more self-confident since she began playing hockey. "The padding helps," she said.

Hockey has also brought Matczynski closer to her family. Her mom comes to Ice games. So do her best friend, her cousins, and her brother. "They like to see women get aggressive," she said. "And we usually all go out to dinner after."

Marcy Bright's family, on the other hand, or at least her mother, thinks she spends too much time with hockey, "whether I'm playing, reffing, or watching other games." This photojournalist from Aurora, Illinois, joined the Chicago Ice in 1996, but she said her mom doesn't see the point, "since I'm kind of old. If I were younger, then she would see that my goal would be to make the U.S. Women's National Hockey Team, compete in the Olympics, or form a professional women's hockey league.

"I was supposed to be an Olympic figure skater," said Bright. "I quit at age 11 after eight years of training." Her brother and father are both very athletic. Although her father was never a hockey fan, he played Triple-A baseball and in college was a star in football, basketball, and baseball. Bright played softball and basketball in college and was offered a scholarship to a small college, but she did not accept it. "Surprisingly, most of my friends are not very athletic!"

Jealousy is what prompted Bright to join the Chicago Ice. "One of my colleagues mentioned she played hockey on a men's team and a women's team. I didn't know how to play the game, but I could skate. I went to the library and read up on the game." Bright also took an instructional hockey clinic before she joined the Chicago Ice. Bright plays on the B squad once or twice a week, but she spends a lot more time on the ice on her own.

"Everything else seems so boring to me now," said Bright. "What my mom (and most people, for that matter) fail to understand is that hockey is an addiction far worse than any drug. I can't explain it. I'm hooked. I can't explain how I'm playing it now when I never cared for the sport as a kid—or an adult—until I was 29! I'd love to play this game as long as I live! Is that nutty or what? I dream of forming a senior citizen's team. If we keep ourselves in shape, I believe it can be done."

Has Bright been hurt? "Put it this way: I'm getting to the point where I'm excelling at the sport and my opponents hate me for it. Hence, no-check hockey has become check hockey, and my body pays dearly for it!" Bright does not let fear of injury hamper her. "I sacrifice my body for the love of the game." She does believe in strength training and stretching. "Tiger balm helps, too," she said.

"My self-confidence has skyrocketed," said Bright, "which has helped my game tremendously. It took a while, but finally, it's there. I owe it all to my coaches."

Bright has the advantage of carrying her love of the game into work, too. She has worked for the Chicago-area *Daily Herald* for seven years and photographs "almost everything you see in the paper from news to features to sports." Naturally, her favorite subject to shoot is sports, "since it's my strongest talent photographically. And of course, the Blackhawks, as poor a team as they are, are still a favorite to photograph." Bright is too busy to socialize much at work, but she said, "I think I'm admired because I play—at least by the sportswriters."

Her family, on the other hand, rarely sees Bright except on the ice during hockey season. "My mom feels my priority should be marriage. Right now, it's hockey." Bright's mom worries about her biological clock. "She thinks my time spent in hockey rinks is a waste of time. Basically, she's ready for grandchildren, is what it comes down to. But luckily, it seems my brother will be tying the knot soon, so maybe I'm off the hook for now." Bright said her mom has been scanning the personals for the past 10 years looking for "what she thinks is the perfect man for me. And, of course, I've obliged and gone out with a few guys. But what she thinks is perfect for me and what I want out of a relationship are two completely different things. Anyway, I'd love to find love at the ice rink, and find a man who appreciates the game of hockey like I do. Because right now, this game means a lot to me, and I'd like to share the love of the game with the love of my life." And it would make her mom happy, too.

Jen Stitzell did find love at the ice rink when a new assistant coach came to the Chicago Ice, but more on that later.

"It [hockey] completely changed my life," said Stitzell, who joined the Ice at age 23, after spending the last three years of college playing hockey and making new friends. Stitzell said her self-image "has changed 100 percent. Playing hockey has changed my life in every conceivable way."

Stitzell, like her dad, has always been a fan of the Chicago Blackhawks, but she did not know of any women's teams. "Girls never played, so I never thought I would play." However, at a game at the University of Chicago, Stitzell saw a woman in the audience wearing a jacket with the name of a women's ice hockey team, and she went over and asked about it. This was her first inkling that women could play ice hockey.

Stitzell couldn't even skate, but the idea didn't go away. "I'll never do this," she thought. "I never took a chance on anything," she said. Nevertheless, she went shopping for skates. There was free skate time at the University of Chicago rink, and she skated five times a week. "In two or three months I could stand," she said, laughing, "but I could not skate backwards. I have no natural athletic ability, but I worked hard and learned." Stitzell believes her mental attitude makes up for whatever she lacks as an athlete. "I know the game really well."

Stitzell has never been hurt on the hockey rink, even though she is a small-framed woman, five feet six, and weighs 125 pounds. Some people tell her, "I cannot believe you play hockey." She laughed. "They don't expect it from me." Stitzell wears all the standard equipment to avoid pain, "but I don't play afraid, and I'm not afraid of pain or of getting hurt. However," she admitted, "I'm afraid to go public skating without padding."

Stitzell said people at work don't understand her passion for hockey. "They say it's ridiculous to play hockey. They just don't have a strange passion." When Stitzell has to take time off from work for a tournament, she tells them, "This is my religion. I tell them they have theirs, this is mine." And on her desk is her 10-inch-high hockey championship trophy to emphasize her point.

What Stitzell enjoys most about playing on the team are "the great people and all the great friends that support me in every way. I also enjoy how we bond with our opponents, who have been through the same discrimination and been laughed at by men for playing 'their' sport. It's something only women athletes would ever understand."

~

Stitzell's B squad lost that final game after the pizza lunch by one point, but in the two years since, they have won every tournament they've played. Chicago Ice teams traveled to Brampton, Ontario, in April of 1999 to participate in the largest women's hockey tournament in the world. In 1999 they won a regional division championship, something they repeated in 2000. Since 1998, the Ice has hosted its own annual Black and Blue Tournament with the help of local business sponsors; it attracts more than a dozen teams from the Midwest and Canada. They have needed two indoor ice surfaces—Johnny's Ice House in Chicago and Heartland Ice Arena in Lincolnwood, Illinois—to accommodate the surge in attendance over the previous years.

In 1999 Ice squads A and B faced each other in the Women's Amateur Hockey Association of Illinois, placing, of course, first and second in the state. The championship banners hang proudly at Johnny's Ice House. The A squad went on to compete in the regional tournament, narrowly losing to St. Louis.

Players from all three Ice squads have appeared in the local and national news, and tournaments have been covered in the *Chicago Tribune* and other sports media. The Ice has emerged from a vision that every woman who wants to play ice hockey should have a place to do so.

Gutowski believes these successes have helped the teams pull together and become more competitive, as she envisioned. "We now consist of multiple squads and are dedicated to assisting each member develop to her fullest potential in skill level, knowledge, and enjoyment of the game," Gutowski said. "This year [2000] we beat our arch rivals [Illinois Storm]," she bragged. "This was a huge victory, 2–0." In the past, the Ice lost by one goal.

"It was such a great experience. And we got trophies," Stitzell said, "big trophies of real women hockey players, and I keep it on my desk at work. It was one of the best moments of my hockey life."

Mary Gutowski got married along the way and in 2000 gave up the Chicago Ice leadership, although she continues to play. She wants to devote more time to rehabbing her new house with her husband. Since the beginning, she has gotten a master's degree in exercise physiology and also works as a personal trainer. She coaches girls in high school and now works in pharmaceutical sales.

"My personal victory," Gutowski said, "is, finally, the idea that a woman can have a family, a career, and also be a competitive athlete. Finally we were able to reach deep down for a common goal."

When Gutowski was a child, her mom would drive her and her siblings to music lessons, but if she wanted to play sports, she was told by her mom, "you'll have to get your own ride."

It looks like she did just that.

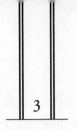

3

THE NEW SOCCER MOMS

~

*"I'll be honest: it feels very strange to have been so abruptly displaced
as the hip sports parent, the one who leads by example and whose
tactical advice has greater weight. Strange, but equally thrilling to know
that my sons now recognize their soccer mom as someone who
packs serious clout, along with the game-day snacks."*

—HARVEY ARANTON, ABOUT HIS WIFE'S SOCCER TEAM,
NEW YORK TIMES, MAY 23, 1999

IT IS THREE O'CLOCK ON A SUNDAY afternoon in July. In 98-degree
heat on a soccer field in suburban Philadelphia, eight women cut
the sleeves off each other's royal blue T-shirts so more air can cir-
culate around their bodies. The shirt logo, a white soccer ball, says,
"Women's Soccer: Women with Balls." Team captain Susan Huot-
Singer, 43, a nurse massage therapist from Phoenixville, Pennsylvania, arrives in an unmatched blue shirt.

"I think one of my kids took it," she explains about her inability
to find her team shirt. Meanwhile, two players leaving the previous
game on the field make a chair with their arms to carry their injured
goalie to a shady spot under the only tree in sight.

As other blues arrive, they pile their sports bags on the grass
along with jug-sized water bottles, ice packs, and towels. Mary
McNichol, 46-year-old assistant director of information systems

at Thomas Jefferson University Medical Center in Philadelphia, pours water over her arms before the game. She took four ibuprofen tablets an hour and a half earlier to blunt potential pain and now swallows two more. "That's the trouble with age," she says cheerfully.

The opposing yellow team enters the field with an entourage of adults and kids carrying folding chairs, coolers, and umbrellas. This team also has a coach on the sidelines, something the blue team does not have. Before the blue and yellow game, the referee, a thin man in black shorts and striped shirt, comes by to say all shin guards must be on and all jewelry off.

"Hey, we gotta talk strategy," Huot-Singer says, drawing the blues around. "I'll play whatever," one player says, as positions are assigned. Team members often play where they are most needed, especially when they don't know much about their opponents' style of play before a game.

"Take off the jewelry," the ref repeats. "Oh, sorry." The player who had been in the huddle and forgotten she was wearing a neck chain unhooks it.

At the whistle, the game begins and the women charge up and down the field at breakneck pace, oblivious to the searing heat. These soccer players, most in their 30s and 40s, with a few 20-somethings, are on the King of Prussia Women's Soccer Team, which is part of the Tri-County Women's Soccer League. They play at least one competitive game a week and sometimes more. They play all year because they can go indoors for the winter games. Summer games include two 20-minute halves with a five-minute break. Indoor games are 40 minutes with no break.

About halfway through the first 20-minute half, a blue player, supported by two others, hops off the field. She has been kicked in the ankle, which was already taped from a previous injury. She is concerned that it might be sprained, but it is just sore. People offer ice packs from their bags.

"It just hurts so bad when you get slammed. I never played center before," she says. After a few minutes with the ice, she returns to the game.

Everyone on the blue team has been injured. Huot-Singer suffered a foot injury from being kicked. Another player has had 13 leg injuries. Mary Ellen Mellor, 45, a sales rep and a high school girls' varsity coach, has broken an arm twice and ruptured her Achilles tendon, not to mention her bad knees. Mellor said she takes Motrin and stretches and uses ice to deal with pain. She admitted that occasionally fear of injury may affect her play, but it doesn't stop her because she loves not only the game but "the wonderful feeling of being part of a team—belonging." Gail Lipstein, 48, didn't even let breast cancer keep her out of the game.

At halftime, the field clears, and the overheated players head for water. They pull water bottles and Gatorade from their bags on the sidelines. A short blonde woman takes a portable battery-operated fan/sprayer from her bag and douses herself and nearby others. The women commiserate with their injured teammate: "Did she hurt you? We'll get her!" They all laugh. Despite the heat, their ragtag appearance, and flushed faces, they don't look tired, but rather energized with joy. They are leading 1–0.

"We gotta stop bunching," one player says.

"If we win, we play again at 6:15."

"Well, that's motivation to lose." They all laugh some more.

"I really, really want us to win this game," repeats the player who does not appreciate the joke and wants the team to be in the play-offs.

In the second half McNichol trips in a scramble for the ball and goes down hard, hitting her head. She blacks out for a moment while both teams crowd around. A teammate presents a bag of Advil from which McNichol takes two. As she is helped from the field, she drinks water and puts ice on her head. The game nearly over, McNichol does not go back in, although she seems unfazed by her injury.

~

This soccer team in Pennsylvania represents what millions of American women are doing—joining amateur soccer teams for the sheer joy of playing the game. Most, like the King of Prussia players, also have full-time families and jobs—but they wouldn't dream of missing a game. A New York State Supreme Court judge told a *New York Times* reporter she had watched her sons play in youth leagues and one day realized how much she would like to put on a uniform and score goals herself. The judge joined a recreational league sponsored by an Irish pub in the Bronx. Her team calls itself the Parlour Moms, and the players have an average age of 45.

The Soccer Industry Council of America estimates that 7.2 million females participated in soccer in 1996. Approximately 40 percent of United States soccer players are girls and women.

Since the Women's World Cup soccer championship in 1999, soccer has become *the* women's team sport. Skill is more important than height and strength, but you also need stamina and endurance. It's about running rather than violence and contact. It's also a social game, and there's easy access to playing surfaces, especially in suburbia with its open fields that can be borrowed or rented from the schools. Soccer is more affordable than a sport like ice hockey with its expensive equipment and ice time rentals. The King of Prussia women pay about $50 a season to cover the cost of referees and their team shirts. They buy their own shoes and shin guards, but these are fairly modest one-time expenses. Total costs average about $400 a year for those playing both the indoor and outdoor seasons.

"I FEEL LIKE A KID AGAIN"

Mary McNichol loves to play soccer. One of her best moments, she said, "was early on [during the first year] when during a game I realized here I am at 45, and I can still learn a new sport and actually play and compete. The whole soccer experience has made me feel more like 'me.' " She said she felt like the person she was in her teens, "when the possibilities were endless and I felt powerful and effective and really liked the way I looked 'cause I was big and strong and in shape." McNichol had played basketball in high school and college but had since drifted away from team sports, relying on running and sporadic visits to a health club to stay fit until her friend Gail Lipstein told her about the soccer team.

McNichol said her competitive spirit got a workout in her first summer of soccer when her sister Antoinette brought her All–New England soccer star daughter to the game and McNichol played to impress her. "The game was a good one, and I played well," she said, although there was no guarantee. "Something I have noticed with sports at my age is that my level of consistency is not there. Some days I feel great and play well; other days I feel tentative, and it really shows."

Many women have cited the particular "flow" of team sports as one of the benefits. Antoinette McNichol, two years older than her sister, played basketball in college as well as 20 years of club field hockey. "One very important part of sports for me was the feeling of 'flow.' It involves us. Flow is being lost to self in something absorbing, exciting, interesting, and challenging."

Catherine Love, a stay-at-home mom from Berwyn, Pennsylvania, said that playing soccer is "the only time that I am not thinking about child-care issues, family matters, work. It is my time, and I play for me and for my team. Afterward I am refreshed, recharged, jazzed, and ready to pick up at home where I left off. Everybody is happier!" Love believes playing soccer has given her a healthy way to relieve stress.

"I have always been athletic and looked athletic. At 42, I am proud to be playing soccer and more comfortable with my self-image than ever before. I feel like a kid again."

It wasn't until Gail Lipstein was 42 that she began to play soccer, although she had been involved in children's soccer for several years. It was through the children's division that she heard about the adult team. She agreed to come to a game one Sunday and fill in for an absent player.

"I was not sure I would qualify for a competitive team," she said. But she did. "It's really fun. All those feelings come back," said Lipstein, who played sports throughout her childhood and college. "It's a struggle. My mind knows what it wants my body to do, but my body doesn't always want to do it."

Lipstein is sorry she didn't have soccer available to her sooner. After college and while she was working as a physical therapist, she played with a softball team for three seasons, but there really wasn't much else available.

"I was always team oriented," Lipstein said. "Other sports like tennis or skiing required instruction, and we didn't have the money for that." As a child, Lipstein played whatever was available at school: field hockey, basketball, softball. She grew up in Stroudsberg, Pennsylvania, in the Poconos as the oldest child, or what she thinks her father considered the "first boy." He played catch with her, and both parents encouraged sports, even if just by driving her to games. Her sister, 18 months younger, played sports only because she felt "she had to compete with me," Lipstein laughed. "I found this out much later."

In her sophomore year at the University of Pennsylvania, where she met Mary McNichol, Lipstein discovered lacrosse, which she had never heard of before. "I absolutely loved it," Lipstein recalled. "Lacrosse put field hockey to shame," she said. She got to be the goalie and went on to become All-Philadelphia and a member of the U.S. National team. She played at the club level for a while after college, but marriage, work, and family took up most of her time. Her lacrosse equipment got packed away in the attic where she recently discovered it, dried up and rotted.

When she was diagnosed with breast cancer, Lipstein wouldn't let it keep her out of the game for long. She had a mastectomy in March 1999, and although she officially took the spring soccer season off, she did not stop. Lipstein's doctors told her not to play soccer for three months, but she bounced back pretty quickly. Because the cancer was in multiple sites of her breast, she needed to have a mastectomy. However, the cancer had not spread beyond her breast, so she did not need to undergo chemotherapy or radiation treatment, which would have made her tired or weak. She had breast reconstruction and is taking medication to prevent any recurrence.

"I was just going to the instructional things [two morning clinics], playing around, coaching, and after six weeks got back into the game as goalie. I was more useful there until I had more endurance." Actually, Lipstein was most concerned about her knees, which have always been bad, so she wears braces.

∼

The blues won their game on that hot July Sunday and went on to face another team in the finals. McNichol bragged about how they beat a younger and faster team.

"We won the 1999 semifinals against a much younger, truly 'trash talking' team. Most of us were so tired from playing all day, and being mostly over 38 we don't have the 'must win at all cost' attitude of youth. So, until we began play, most of us didn't care too much if we won. But when the team was so gratuitously rough and foul-mouthed, our team developed a collective resolve just to beat them, which we did. And we were thrilled. It was like high school again—the sheer joy of winning and pride at having beaten a tough team."

~

Months later, on the coldest night of the next winter, the team played another winning game, this one inside. McNichol prefers the indoor soccer they play in winter because it's a smaller field, and thus, a rougher game. She talks of "scoring three goals in an indoor game—just one of those times when everything you do is just right."

The arena in King of Prussia, Pennsylvania, called Rocket Sports, looks like two hockey rinks inside a tennis bubble. The floor is covered with AstroTurf, and a yellow strip defines the beginning of a white wooden wall that goes halfway up and is completed with Plexiglas. The arena is in constant use on weekends with two games (men's and women's) going on at once. Players and spectators hang around the snack bar, which is up on a balcony for those who can tolerate some mediocre pizza or a hot dog. Husbands, boyfriends, and children lean over the railing and watch the action below. Video machines line the back wall—one reason McNichol's son Travis, 12, comes more often to watch his mom's indoor games. A few rows of bleacher seats stand in front of Plexiglas walls around the rink. A couple of preteen boys kick a soccer ball back and forth along the floor in front of the bleachers.

Travis thinks his mom is "definitely weird" to play soccer at her age, but after watching her play, he told her for the first time ever that he was proud of her. McNichol's daughter Callie, 14, who plays basketball in high school but hates the "Women with Balls" logo, is not without a sense of humor. She asked her mother after one game, "If you had to choose between being an athlete and my mother, which would you choose?"

Team captain Huot-Singer said that her playing soccer has brought a depth to her relationship with her son "that would have never been there otherwise. At 14, teenagers don't want to talk to their moms," she said. "It's still tough, but I know from what teachers and his middle school soccer coach told me that my son is proud of the fact that I play and coach. I would never have known this if they hadn't shared it with me, but it makes me different, and I think that he likes that. I just love being able to see what he sees in a game, to be as excited about the game. Maybe I'm full of it, but after hearing the coach and teachers, I think it does make a difference. We can talk about soccer, being a team player, being a human being in the game of life. It brings us to a common ground."

Catherine Love's four-year-old son always warns her as she leaves for a game or practice, "Don't head the ball, don't fall down, and be careful."

4

ROLLIN' ON THE RIVER

~

"Rowing is absolute teamwork. There are no stars in the boat,
and that is why I like it so much."

—Virginia Amos

I<small>T IS A DARK AND DRIZZLY PREDAWN</small> October morning on the Potomac River, and Virginia Amos is the eighth person in the boat. All she can see is the back of the rower in front of her. On the T-shirt are the words, "Just sit down and row." She has forgotten her gloves this morning, so her fingers are cold.

"I started rowing because I had just turned 50 and wanted to give this to myself," says Amos, a publisher's representative who discovered a large rowing community in Alexandria, Virginia, where she lives. "I had never done it before." Amos joins her teammates every weekday at 5:30 A.M. when the river is free of traffic. "And I was never a morning person," she says.

"The hardest thing is smooshing in my contacts at 5 A.M.," Amos says. "My eyes are all grainy and scratchy." Amos, who wears no makeup, laughs and says, "There's no vanity here, although I've seen Roxie come in with eye makeup."

Each morning the eight women of the team lift the $200,000 scull from the overhead rack in the boathouse, a large and impressive loftlike building, and together carry it out to the water. The boat is 58 feet long and weighs more than 200 pounds.

"And when it's over, we carry it back," Amos says. They also carry out the launch, in which their coaches ride. Someone cleans the ramp so they don't slip. "The ducks are the worst hazard," Amos says, recounting a story of a man who slipped on the duck poop and was out cold. "An ambulance carted him away to the hospital."

"Rowing is absolute teamwork," says Amos. "There are no stars in the boat, and that is why I like it so much." Everyone has to row with the same stroke, for the same amount of time. An experienced recreational crew should average about 32 strokes a minute. Olympic teams reach about 38 strokes.

These rowers are "sweeping"; that is, each uses one oar on the opposite side of the boat as the rowers in front and behind. In sculling, each rower uses two oars. Because of the sensitive balance of the boat, every shift or misstroke can cause it to rock. If one person is leaning a little the wrong way, it will throw everyone off or water can come into the boat. When the rowers were swamped once, the coach shouted from the launch, "Just keep rowing," and tossed Amos a quart-size container, like an old milk bottle, to bail. "And suddenly water was up to my chest." The launch raced over and pulled each rower out.

～

Karen Snyder, a special education teacher in the Alexandria public schools, enjoys being the coxswain, the only person in the boat who can see where they are going. The women take turns at this. The coxswain communicates via headset and microphone to speakers at strategic locations in the boat. The challenge is to remain in charge, remain balanced.

"If a rower so much as turns her head, it could set the keel off," Snyder said. "If you catch a crab, this means the oar hits the water wrong and the rower behind you gets hit with the oar, or worse, the boat flips over."

There are all kinds of perils related to rowing. Snyder recalled a time when "a big fish jumped into the boat and everyone began screaming. The launch came over, and the coach tried to get [the fish] out of the boat with an oar. Because of the way the boat is constructed, the women could not stop rowing, or even remove their feet from their position. Otherwise they would capsize the boat."

Shoes, mostly sized to fit men, are nailed into the bottom of the boat so the rower can slip her foot into position. Amos told of a short woman whose "shoes" were too far from her body and she flipped out of the boat. The launch came right away and fished her out.

"Sometimes river rats get up on the boat. There are all kinds of things floating," Snyder said. We have to watch for wrecks, sunken stuff, even the foam channel markers. Some places are pretty shallow, and the rudder can run aground. We lost our rudder once and had to tie it with strings. You can steer with the oars, but you need a rudder. Sometimes we get caught in the weeds.

"There is a large safety factor," she said. "It could be dark, or stormy. We have only running lights. We have to be quiet, follow the river patterns. There's a lot of traffic with other rowers. We could get run down, but there's not much river traffic at that hour.

"[Traffic] gets to be a serious problem in summer when there are many more novices and kids who cut across your path," said Snyder, who signed up with the adult learn-to-row program because she saw how turned on her kids were about rowing.

Rhonda Taylor, 33, said she actually fell in the river with an earlier rowing club. "We were doing a standing shove off the dock. I wasn't used to getting into the boat this way, so when we shoved off, I lost my balance and fell into the Anacostia River. The funny part was that I was in the bow [front] and my splash was kind of quiet, so no one knew that I had fallen in, except the person in front of me [whose back was to her]. Everyone, except for [the number] two seat kept rowing as I tried to get back in the boat. The water was ice cold, and so was the air outside. I just wanted to get in my car and go home, but in the end, one of the rowers gave me some sweatpants, and I did a quick change."

"A lot of times my friends ask me how I can get up so early to row in the morning," Taylor said. "The thrill of watching the sunrise on the water and the way my body feels after a nice strenuous practice," is what keeps her coming to the Potomac. "It's like time is suspended and all the noise caused by the airplanes at National Airport and the cars traveling over the Wilson Bridge are absorbed by the sun's brilliance. First there is a brightness that breaks the morning's darkness. Then, slowly, the sky changes colors, and as you look to the east a red glow starts to break above the horizon. In a way, this seems to empower me. The warmth feels good against my skin and is comforting. As we row into the sun and the rates pick up there is just a feeling that I can do anything. And as the sweat rolls off my forehead and down into my eyes, and as my chest heaves for air, I feel alive and invigorated."

Snyder agreed, "It's a great way to work out. It gives you a jolt in the morning, and it's a fluid motion." The rowers are home by 7:00 to get ready to go to work. On Saturday they begin an hour later, at 6:30, and then go out to breakfast together. The rowers also get together for dinner every month and keep in touch via E-mail. They invite each other to parties at their homes and work out together.

"We have fun," Snyder said. Nobody likes to miss a session on the water because they cannot take out the boat unless everyone is there. "It lets the others down," Snyder said.

The Alexandria rowers are part of a tight-knit community where rowing has been a tradition for a very long time. They are lucky to have a good clubhouse—part of the high school rowing program— which gets special funding. Everyone chips in and helps with the new boathouse addition or with maintenance of boats and equipment. For example, 60 people might show up to paint the oars.

THAT THING CALLED SWING

Rowing, with its need for synchronicity and its early hour, is like a ballet or chorus. It strengthens the body and relaxes the mind, and many rowers enjoy the sport for its meditative quality. There is no running or jumping, and you don't need any particular skill except a sense of grace and rhythm so you are in sync with the rest of the rowers.

This repetitive and intense effort can be a form of meditation. There's only the rhythm, like a mantra. The effortless condition, when everything falls into place, is known as "swing." This transcendent state or zone is what hooks many rowers. Amos described the great feeling, "when we are all rowing well, on-keel, swooshing down the river at dawn."

Taylor said one of her best moments on the water was in a race in Philadelphia. "I was in a four with some of my friends. We were all novices and thrown together kind of last minute, but the way we rowed that race, one would have thought we had rowed together for ages. We put so much effort into it. At one point I started to kind of grunt, but according to the stories of the rest of that boat, it was more of a moan. Anyway, it got everyone else motivated, and we started to really move, and in the end we won our heat. The stories that followed, though, were not really of our victory but of the totally 'orgasmic' experience we had while rowing."

Dancing is another metaphor that has been used when describing rowing. Ernestine "Ernie" Bayer, who started the Philadelphia Girls' Rowing Club in 1938, told a reporter, "My boat is my partner, and it's like dancing on the water. It's the best way to describe it— rhythm, rhythm. That's what rowing is."

Half the women responding to a survey about why they row mentioned the rhythm and grace of rowing. Cited most often as the reason for rowing was friendship and camaraderie, followed by mental and physical challenges, health and fitness, and love of being on the water.

The Row As One Camp, the first masters rowing camp for women, publishes a newsletter, *Reach*, that reported the results of a survey on "why do masters women row?" For the 55 respondents to the survey, the average age is 46, and the women have been rowing for an average of seven years. More than half the women have been rowing for two to five years. Primary motives include developing physical strength through rowing and experiencing teamwork. Nearly all (93 percent) are competitive rowers, and 85 percent consider rowing their primary sport.

∼

Although summer is best, the women in Alexandria row until late October. "We work up a sweat soon, but our fingers get chilled," Amos said. Once it's too cold to go out on the water, they work out at the boathouse.

"The music is cranked up, and 35 women are working," said Amos about her first workout of bench presses, sit-ups, leg presses, and other organized exercises to develop the strong legs and thighs needed for rowing. The first five days she felt great, but over the weekend, when her muscles had a chance to relax, she said, "I thought I would die." Amos, never a morning person, admitted she has been tempted to stay under the covers on some dark winter mornings. "But whenever I did that, I felt lousy all day." She enjoys the feeling of accomplishment she gets from being part of something that is very different from her "normal" life.

Rowing is a sport anyone can learn, and it's the fastest growing team sport. The physical demand is on the large leg and arm muscles as well as the torso. For rowing, tall is good for balance. Long arms help rowers get a good long stroke. Uniformity is important for better speed.

For the rowers, the winter workouts are not as competitive as the workouts in the boat. "I don't need the top erg score," Snyder said. "Your erg [rowing ergometer] score is used to judge your ability, but it is not a judge of team rowing."

~

Before baseball captured the American sports imagination, rowing was the most popular spectator sport in the country. The greatest fans were men of the working class who lined the banks of the Potomac River in Washington, D.C., the Charles River in Boston, and the Schuylkill River in Philadelphia in the 1800s to watch celebrities row for prize money. Gambling and drinking were part of the appeal and led to a ban on professional rowing in 1896. Rowing retreated to the Ivy League, where it developed a more "elite" image.

Although women have been rowing since the 1800s, they were allowed only a light paddle and a short race—nothing like today's collegiate scene. When Ernestine Bayer started her club, women began racing, but it wasn't until the 1960s that women organized into The National Women's Rowing Association. And their Olympic debut didn't happen until 1976 in Montreal. Even then, their races were only 1,000 meters instead of the standard 2,000.

While college women were allowed to row, they never got the same equipment, facilities, or support as men. Women at Yale staged an effective protest and lawsuit in 1976, which has been immortalized in the 1999 documentary film *A Hero for Daisy* by Mary Mazzio. It portrays two-time Olympian Chris Ernst, who galvanized her rowing team to storm the Yale athletic director's office to protest the lack of locker-room facilities for women.

~

Snyder's daughter, Rebecca, 21, is a junior at Brown, which has the number one women's rowing team. Rebecca began to crew in eighth grade in the Alexandria learn-to-row program and she is now a champion rower. Snyder's son, 18, is about to go to college and doesn't know if he will continue rowing or focus on track and field.

"I don't think they know how well I row," Snyder said about her kids. They also may not know that she picks up some tips from her daughter's coaches. "I pick the brain of the Brown University coach," Snyder said. While coaches from the Alexandria boathouse accompany the women each morning, Snyder doesn't think they are always helpful.

"Some coaches are not nice," Snyder said. "They create tension. I don't want to be uptight at 5:30 in the morning."

What these rowers do want is that thing called swing.

5

AT THE HOOP: WHO SAYS GRANDMAS CAN'T JUMP?

~

"We were overlooked as champions way back in '54;
The guys got all the scholarships; we got to sweep the floor.
But now we're back again to try to even up the score.
Our team goes marching on."

—WORDS BY MAVIS ALBIN, TO THE TUNE OF
"BATTLE HYMN OF THE REPUBLIC"

O NE MORNING IN 1992, as Mavis Albin, then 55, leaned against her kitchen island reading the Baton Rouge, Louisiana, *Advocate*, a news item about the Senior Olympic Games caught her attention.

"You know," she said casually to her husband, Joe, when he came into the room, "I would love to play basketball again." Joe, a tall, handsome man who loves sports almost as much as he loves Mavis, said, "Why don't you?" That was all it took for Mavis Albin to get back into the game she so loved to play in high school. Then, Mavis McMorris had been one of the best guards on the Doyle High School girls' basketball team, such as it was in the days when only forwards could shoot the ball. Albin called the National Senior Games representative in Baton Rouge, who invited her to a practice being held not far away. The rest, as they say, is history.

Now known as the Louisiana Tigerettes Hi-Tops, Albin and the rest of her team have won gold medals in the United States Senior Olympics in 1998, 1999, and 2000. They have played and won against younger women and against men. They played an exhibition game with the Houston Comets, traveled across the country, appeared on national television, and had their photo taken in the Louisiana state senate, where they were recognized as National Senior Olympics champs. They are not only playing ball; they are having a ball.

"In my very first National Senior Olympics we played at Louisiana State University," Albin said. "I was fortunate enough to hit a three-pointer that resulted in us winning the gold medal in our age division. I remember we did not hear the buzzer and were all still playing, and one of my teammates jumped off the bench onto the floor, grabbed the ball, and shouted, 'The game is over; we won!'"

Albin could barely contain her excitement. "Sportswriters doing interviews, TV cameras, sponsors hugging us, and the opposing team MAD! My grandsons were there, and it was a thrill to hear them shout, 'Come on, Maw Maw.'

"We were pleased that we were still conscious; however, when I returned home and began to get out of the car I was moaning," Albin said. "My family was there to greet me, and I could hardly walk. I was dragging my feet. I honestly could not lift them. My legs were sore, my ankles were swollen, my back hurt, and my fingers were stiff. My kids and grandsons thought this was so funny. I worked hard to get in shape, and I never felt like that again," Albin said. "At first I was exhausted in two minutes," she recalled. "Now I play the whole game and feel great."

Six months before a tournament season starts, the team begins serious conditioning. Albin outlined a typical day.

"We jogged around the church gym and then went to the YMCA and spent another hour working on the machines, the treadmill, the bike, weights. Then we'd play for an hour. The stamina comes. The energy comes," Albin said. "We've played as many as four games in one day." When other women Albin's age come up to her and say, "I wish I could do that," she tells them, "Just go out and play."

Of her teammates Albin said, "They want to play so badly they come out limping. We pad our feet, we brace our knees, we wrap our fingers, and rub our elbows, all because we want to play basketball," Albin said. "We would never think of doing that for spring cleaning."

The Tigerettes Hi-Tops are always looking for a more intense workout and often scrimmage with the Louisiana State University women's team or with players at the local Y.

"We played the men at the YMCA," Albin said. "These were young guys. At first whenever they'd bump into us they'd say, 'Oh, sorry.' Then they saw how aggressive the Tigerettes were, and they didn't cut [us] any slack. You can play real rough with the guys."

"Most teams come out timid against them," said Lanette Albin, Mavis's daughter-in-law, "but after four or five minutes, they change their minds." Because Mavis Albin was a guard in her high school games, and thus never did any shooting, she asked her daughter-in-law to teach her to shoot a one-handed jump shot. She said, "I had limited experience shooting, especially with one hand."

"She can knock the bottom out of it now," said Lanette, who went to college on a basketball scholarship and still plays recreationally and with her children, as well as occasionally coaching her mother-in-law's team.

The competitive spirit runs deep in the Tigerettes Hi-Tops, but recently Albin let her soft heart get in the way of that spirit when she told a competing player to "get the ball, and I won't guard you." Teammate Nikki Leader hollered, "Mavis, if you're gonna play like that, get off the floor." Albin said she just wanted the player to know how good it felt to score. When Leader, who is a big competitor, later said she was only kidding, Albin responded emphatically, "No, you weren't."

~

Soon after Albin went to that first practice, she and two other women became the Baton Rouge Tigerettes, named for their favorite women's basketball team, the Louisiana State University Tigers. The new athletes went to their first tournament.

"I was told about the State Tournament of Senior Olympics three-on-three half-court basketball. Two other ladies and myself formed a team," Albin said. The Tigerettes had no "bench," so each player played all four games back-to-back. At the time, Albin said, "The rule was if someone called a time-out the clock continued to run. When they would get ahead they would call time-out and let the clock run. That rule has since been changed."

Albin's daughter-in-law, Lanette, was coaching the Tigerettes, "and she kept saying, 'Don't you want to forfeit this last game?' I said, 'No, we came to play and we'll play until it's over.' I did not feel like that would be fair to the other teams," Albin said. She admits she was not in great shape. Nevertheless, the Tigerettes won the bronze.

The National Senior Games are bracketed by age, and when Albin turned 60 she chose to stay with the 50-somethings because she wanted a more competitive team. Now known as the Louisiana Tigerettes Hi-Tops, they are undefeated.

The other women who make up the current team are Barbara Avant, 54, a retired physical education teacher of Lafayette, Louisiana; Linda Benge, 56, a housewife, of Livingston, Louisiana; and Kitty Sparacello, 56, of New Orleans, Louisiana, a retired physical education professor at Loyola University. In 1997 two new players joined the team: Nikki Dixon Leader, 53, of Denham Springs,

Louisiana, a junior high school teacher and coach; and her sister, Wanda Blailock, 55, a makeup artist of Jackson, Mississippi. Ironically, Leader would not have had the time to join this team if she had not just lost her high school coaching job for trying to bring equality to girls' sports and achieve equal pay for girls' coaches at Denham Springs High School.

∼

"I love sports," said Avant, who still holds the record in her school for scoring the most points ever—53—in a basketball game. This retired physical education teacher hadn't played in 25 years and thought it would be fun.

"I'm a natural athlete, so it makes it easy," she said. "I feel good about myself. It makes me have a motive for exercising." Avant has had knee surgery in the past and uses a brace. "I do worry about injury," she admitted. "I can't move as well as I want to." But she takes arthritis medications and says that helps.

Benge lost 25 pounds when she joined the Tigerettes Hi-Tops, "because I didn't want to look bad on the court." She laughed about this because she has always been active and bowls regularly, but joining the basketball team inspired the weight loss. "I counted calories," she said about her diet plan. She had learned about the games through Albin, who lives in the same town and went to the same high school.

"I see myself as a more active person," Leader said about her improved self-image. Leader said she's played with fingers bandaged up and she wears knee pads, does stretching exercise, and works out for endurance. Why does she do it? "The love of the game. Being able to play at my age. I always loved this game. This is now really a sport I can play the rest of my life."

~

In the early years, the Louisiana Tigerettes Hi-Tops pretty much paid their own way for uniforms and to travel to competitive games, mostly by driving thousands of miles. But gradually, they have attracted the help of some sponsors. And it was a good thing, because the team kept winning, which meant traveling to more competitions.

Gerry Lane Chevrolet in Baton Rouge was the team's first sponsor and picked up the tab for uniforms and travel. Now, the arthritis medication Osteo-Bi-Flex, manufactured by Rexall, is also providing support, which helps bring down costs. They sent the Tigerettes Hi-Tops new suits, bags, and warm-ups and promised additional shirts and shoes were on the way.

It was through Leader's involvement with LSU players that the Tigerettes got their cool high-top shoes. Katrina Hibbert, a starter for LSU and now a starting forward for the WNBA Seattle Storm, is a friend of Leader's daughter. One day, Hibbert gave an extra pair of her basketball shoes to Leader, a big fan of the Louisiana State University women's basketball team who never misses a home game and sees most away games as well.

"I suppose she did not need the purple and gold shoes, so she gave them to Nikki to give to someone," Albin said. That someone with the big foot [size 10] happened to be me. That's one time a big foot was nice. Nikki asked me if I would like to have them, and I was like a big kid. I loved them.

"I mentioned to Nikki that we needed to get some shoes for all the team," Albin said. "Nikki told Katrina we would like to buy some if possible. They got shoes for every player. As a courtesy to Katrina and the LSU women's basketball team and coach Sue Gunter, we added 'Hi-Tops' to our name. Sue also gave us a couple of basketballs."

Albin's grandsons also want to walk in her basketball shoes.

"I knew my grandsons would love them; they were new and so wild. One grandson had sports day at school and could wear anything he wanted. He asked me if he could wear those shoes, and even though they were too big, I said sure. That afternoon he said, 'Maw Maw, all the kids wanted these shoes. They thought they were so cool.'

"Everywhere we would go, from the youngest to the senior adults," Albin said, "they would ask me about my shoes. In fact, we were in Houston playing, and a lady asked me where we got our shoes, and I told her they were Louisiana State University shoes. She said, very seriously, 'I have a grandson who is an attorney there and I am going to get him to get me a pair of those.'"

IT'S OUR TIME

The best moment of her new athletic career for Linda Benge came in 1998 in Houston, when the Tigerettes were invited to a half-time scrimmage at a WNBA Comets game.

"At first, it was scary," Benge recalled. There were so many people there compared to 300 at other games they had played. "As soon as I began playing, I forgot about the people there." She said they played for about five or six minutes to cheers from more than 10,000 people in the audience.

"They told us we had some awesome moves," Benge remarked. "People would ask us how did we do it." A few people had negative comments such as, "Don't you know you're too old to do that," or "You're gonna get hurt." Benge said she and the others are not the least bit phased by such comments.

Albin, who follows the Comets religiously, said that day was one of the highlights of her new athletic career, especially since her 16-

year-old grandson went with her to Houston, too. The late Kim Per-rot, the Comets' point guard, who died of cancer in 1999, presented each member of the team with a WNBA basketball.

Albin still marvels at the idea of women getting paid to play bas-ketball. "Women's basketball is so very different now in comparison to the fifties. I was a guard, and all I could do was get the ball to the forward," said Albin, who is five feet eight. "Guards were not allowed to shoot in those days." Nevertheless, her passion for the game kept Albin going through some rough times. When she was a senior in Doyle High School, her mother got very ill and died at the age of 48.

"The only thing that kept me in school was basketball," Albin said of that traumatic time. And if that wasn't enough, the fates gave her a double whammy when the family home burned down. In addi-tion to losing all the family possessions, Albin lost her purple and gold basketball uniform and had to play an important district tour-nament wearing shorts and her number pinned on the back of a T-shirt. "In those days it was no big deal," she said about playing out of uniform. In 1954 the local newspaper caption was so small—"Mavis McMorris, all district"—that it was easily overlooked.

Albin played independently with some other women after grad-uating high school, but there were few opportunities for competitive play, and once her three sons began arriving, she gave it up. She and her husband ran a business together and raised a family.

Albin said, "I would lie awake in my bed at night wondering about the thrill of running full court, dribbling the ball, and shoot-ing. I realized when I played the last game my senior year, that would end my basketball career. There were no scholarships offered to women that I was aware of. No hall of fame, no hanging of uniforms in the gym, no recognition at all.

"I would have thought it only a dream in the fifties to be able to play the sport that I dearly love 40 years after graduating from high school," Albin said. "The spark of competition in sports has been renewed, but winning the National Champion title is certainly a dream come true. I believe winning is much sweeter now than it could ever have been in the fifties."

Sparacello and Avant were inspired by their mothers, both of whom were true pioneers and played basketball. Sparacello's mom, now 83, can cheer her daughter and granddaughter. Avant's mom played basketball and volleyball in high school and touch football in college.

"My mom kept a scrapbook on me during my high school and college years," Avant said. "She passed away in 1999, so I miss not having her to share my highlights with. But my dad is proud. Husband and kids, brothers, also like to hear my game stories." Before she retired, Avant was a physical education teacher and coached the "Little Dribblers" when her kids played. Her husband, also a physical education teacher and coach, had played college basketball. Their daughter Tammy, 30, and son Shayne, 27, both played in high school.

Growing up in the rice country of southwestern Louisiana, Sparacello played in high school and some in college, where she majored in physical education. She coached junior high school while in college, and taught high school. At the college level, she specialized in "lifetime sports" at Central Methodist College and then at Loyola for 10 years. At the time, nobody considered basketball a lifetime sport.

With her professional and family responsibilities, Sparacello put aside her own game, but when she learned there was no basketball team in her daughter's high school, she organized one. One day, her daughter, at the time a senior in high school, saw a news item about the Senior Games and told her mom, "You should do it." Her daughter is now an exchange student in Australia, where she's the leading scorer on the basketball team.

Blailock and Leader came from a family with four girls and one boy and a father who loved sports. Their dad, J.C., a state police captain, was the big influence and never missed any of their games.

"All of my sisters played basketball in high school," Leader said. "All of us were All-District players. Two of us were All-State players. One of my sisters was two-time All-State in high school." After high school, with no college programs available, Leader played in independent basketball and softball clubs for a while.

Blailock likes competition and believes she performs better under stress. Her father always told her, "Do the best you can at whatever you do." She remembers watching her dad play baseball. Her mother was the musical one and got "Wannie" interested in piano and singing. Blailock began voice lessons at 32 and began singing at weddings. Between that and piano practice, she was always busy. At Louisiana State University she won the talent show in 1966. When she married and moved to Mississippi after college, she took up golf.

"We could each do one thing," Blailock said of her childhood and how her family decided which lessons each child could take. She and her sisters, including Leader, chose basketball and were always coached by their dad.

Blailock tore her rotator cuff on the job, and the injury kept her out of the Tigerettes games for a while. It was a tough decision to have surgery for her rotator cuff, because she knew she had to keep her ability to raise her arm high.

"Someone told me that they had rotator cuff surgery and could only raise their arm halfway up. I had to shoot over my head, so until I knew for sure it was torn, I didn't want surgery." But Blailock has some good lessons from the past to help her make that decision. As a child she contracted osteomyelitis and was not expected to walk. Her father sold the family's only cow to pay for treatment. He knew his daughter would be able to walk. Blailock had the rotator cuff surgery and is back in the game.

~

These renewed athletes get plenty of recognition now, including national television coverage. A news crew from ABC-TV came to Louisiana to film the Louisiana Tigerettes Hi-Tops for several days in the spring of 2000.

Albin cooked the crew a real Southern breakfast of grits, cinnamon rolls, sausage, and biscuits. "For something colorful and delicious," Albin said, "I cooked a strawberry float cake. It does just that—floats in a mixture of three pints crushed strawberries, [condensed] milk, and sugar. Topping consists of Cool Whip with two large strawberries on top. The camera crew piled their equipment around the kitchen, and we ate as we visited, standing up. The weather was absolutely beautiful. The sun was shining, the temperature was perfect."

Albin lives in the first house that was built on Joe Albin Drive in Livingston, just east of Baton Rouge. The road is named for her husband because he was once mayor and because they were the first ones to move onto this road in 1960. "We live on 21 acres, and there's a huge oak tree in front. All the very old people tell us they used to swing their girlfriends on a swing hung from that tree. Our home is surrounded by trees on all sides where the sunrays almost look heavenly as they burst through. My husband and I have five pet deer in the pen, and we usually feed them vanilla wafers as a treat. In all our hustle to get everything in and get to the ball game in Harahan with the ABC crew, I am not sure if anyone gave them their cookies."

The ABC producers wanted the Tigerettes Hi-Tops to bring along some photos of themselves and their teams from high school.

"We had a lot of laughs looking over these strange pictures," Albin said. In high school, Linda Benge and her brother were voted best athletes. The ABC crew asked Linda if she resented that there was no program for women in those days. Linda said that in a way she did, but after high school she played in a church league for a few years.

"After high school it was taken away," Albin said on camera. "We feel like it's our time."

Benge was asked how long she was gonna do this. "As long as I can stand," she replied.

On March 27, 2000, during the Final Four March Madness of the NCAA play-offs and a few hours before the Louisiana State University women's team took on the University of Connecticut, the Tigerettes Hi-Tops special aired on ABC-TV with Peter Jennings narrating. The segment, called "Tiger Power at the Hoop," showed the team opposing strong young men and women. As one surprised young man commented about the intensity of the match, "It's a moment I'll never forget."

~

"Women still have to deal with injustice in sports. . . . In Orlando we ran into a very difficult situation during the finals of the tournament," Albin said.

In the middle of the U.S. Senior Olympics Women's Basketball tournament, Tony McDonald, basketball director, changed the playing bracket in the women's 50-plus division. As a result, the number two–place winner in the pool had the advantage over the Tigerettes Hi-Tops, the number one–place winner. The first-place winner should have the advantage, and the unsatisfactory change affected other teams as well.

The players voiced their disagreement about this change, but McDonald would not discuss it with the team. When they requested a policy form to present a written protest, "he was rude and said he didn't have any forms." The Tigerettes learned later that he had lied. Albin's team also knew that the rules said if a team leaves the gym before the written protest is authenticated, they forfeit the right to protest. Because they had no form, team manager Leader wrote a protest on a blank sheet of paper and asked an associate to the basketball director to sign it.

The Tigerettes Hi-Tops then drove to the administrative offices to get protest forms and make sure their grievance was aired. They talked to McDonald's superiors and got the ruling reversed. When they got back to Louisiana, they wrote an official letter of complaint.

Nevertheless, they had fun in Orlando. They spotted Jack Palance, one of the celebrity guests at the games. "He is famous for his one-handed push-up," Albin said, "and we happened to recognize him as he was going to his vehicle. We asked him if he would mind taking a picture with us. He was very gracious and agreed to a photo. We joked with him and presented him with Mardi Gras beads. We laugh and tell everyone he wanted his picture with *us*. Of course they say, 'Yeah, right!' "

"It is a beautiful place of rolling hills," Sparacello said about the area surrounding the Disney World sports facility. "That last game was filled," she said, and all ages were in the audience. "We giggled and cut up like we were in high school," she quipped, "pulling pranks, laughing."

Albin said, "I came home to a big cake my daughters-in-law had made, and they had also made a big banner that covered the end of the den. There was a sign outside of Livingston's local hardware store, too: "Congratulations Gold Medal Winners.""

"MAMA, I NEVER KNEW YOU COULD PLAY LIKE THAT"

Albin's family all love basketball. All of her daughters-in-law play recreational basketball. Her sons, 38, 40, and 41, are proud of her accomplishment. People at the gym tell Albin, "Your sons have been telling us what you're doing."

"Joe is supportive, and so are my sons, daughters-in-law, and especially my six grandsons," said Albin, "but everyone is eager to give me pointers—how to dribble through the legs, behind the back, and shoot a one-handed jump shot.

"I chose the number 5 to be on my uniform shirt because of my five little grandsons. However, here comes another little ray of sunshine, another big boy. His older brother, Aaron, asked, 'Maw Maw, what about your number 5 now that Collin is here?' I could not take the number 6 since another team member had that one, so I told him, we'll fix that. I added five plus one. Aaron was happy that his younger brother was not left out."

Linda Benge's eight grandchildren give her basketballs, and after each road trip they ask her how many medals were won.

"My son had been away in college, and he happened to come to a practice," recalled Sparacello. "He said, 'Mama, I never knew you could play like that. I never knew how good you are.'" Sparacello said she couldn't help but laugh "at the shock on his face."

"My children and family love me being involved," Leader said. "My children think it's great because they love the game and so do I." Leader, who is divorced, admitted that her husband would probably not have been so supportive. Her dad sure would have been proud.

BETTER THAN THERAPY

"All the other teams have a coach, a trainer," Sparacello said. "We are gonna stay the way we are!" Many of these women are or were coaches. "We're very versatile," she said about the Tigerettes Hi-Tops. "We play all positions. We all have a voice."

"We are all sort of bossy," Nikki Leader said. "We get along great, however."

After winning the National Senior Olympics basketball championship in October 1999, the Tigerettes Hi-Tops took some time off for a rest, but they never quit completely. Six months before their yearly tournaments begins, the team starts serious conditioning, getting ready to face their packed schedule and play all around their own state and neighboring states.

"We plan our social lives around our schedule," Albin said. "Nobody connected with the Tigerettes can have a family wedding, birthday, or anything else without consulting the team schedule."

"This is better than therapy," Albin said. "It has done so much for our self-esteem." And it has helped team members get through life's trials and tragedies. "One was going through a divorce and then lost her father. Another's husband lost his job and then her mother died. They've dealt with kids with alcohol or drug problems; we've been through it all." Albin herself had been recovering from the heartbreak of a family tragedy years earlier. Her young pregnant daughter-in-law was killed in an automobile accident by a drunk driver. Playing basketball again was the only thing that helped Albin move past her grief.

"Now it's our time," Albin said.

"It's given us all an incredible lift," Sparacello said, "a renewal. We encourage each other. It's kind of refreshing to realize that basketball is a lifetime sport," she said. "Nobody considered it before. They just assumed you couldn't play that."

"It's the best stress reliever I know," Albin said. "We laugh at each other and at ourselves, and we forget we are senior citizens as we act like teenagers. The other day we were in Montgomery [Alabama], and we took the stairs up to our hotel rooms. We were laughing so hard about something that I sat on the steps and Nikki was in the doorway with her legs crossed. We laughed so hard we hurt." Another day, Leader was hiding behind a counter at the hotel and suddenly jumped out and scared Albin. "I screamed at the top of my lungs," she said, noting some disgruntled hotel guests around them.

Each of the Tigerettes shelled out ten dollars for some fake buck teeth they call "Billy Bob" teeth and walked around town "smiling" at people. "We roll the windows down and ask for directions with our teeth in," Albin said. "We start to sing; that's difficult. We see people laughing and go over to them and ask, 'Are you laughing at me?' They look again and they wonder is this real or not? The baffled looks are what we love. We have had guys say, 'I'm a dentist; would you like my card?' And we say, 'No, we don't have any cavities.' People would turn and say to us, 'It looks like you girls are having fun' as we paraded in front of thousands of people with our newfound teeth.

"My kids cannot believe I did this," Albin said. "We have and are still having a million dollars worth of laughs. Do we have fun? Yes, yes, yes."

~

The Tigerettes Hi-Tops were still undefeated in 2000, but as Albin predicted, "We know defeat is coming, because the teams are getting better and better. But for now, how sweet it is."

Before play begins at each tournament, Albin said, "We bow for a moment of prayer, and I thank God each day that I am able to be on a basketball court."

Blailock said, "Lots of people do not think women should be playing basketball or doing much of anything. They think we should be sitting in a rocking chair. That's for the birds."

Albin wrote a song—sung to the tune of "Battle Hymn of the Republic"—about the bad old days of basketball. She wrote it when they played at a warm-up during the 1997 National Senior Games.

Leader, who sings in the same community choir as Albin, said "Mavis has a beautiful voice."

The second verse is at the head of this chapter, but here is the chorus:

We're back again, hallelujah!
Let's play ball, hallelujah!
We're back again, hallelujah!
To represent the U.S.A.

6

THE GIRLS OF SUMMER

~

"More than 14 million Americans play softball, and half of them are women. In 1996, 11.2 million females played softball, and 2.8 million females played baseball."

—Sporting Goods Manufacturers Association, 1997

"In some respects we're still all kids out there," said Diane Hein, 57, who has played softball two or three times a week since she was 27. "I like getting out and yelling and screaming." Hein likes the sociability, too. "You meet somebody else in a uniform and you talk."

Hein is currently on the California Spirit Majors, a slow-pitch, senior softball team whose members are between the ages of 55 and 72. She plays all positions, but mostly catcher, and she has been on three winning teams in the Senior World Series.

"The seniors use the 11-inch ball, like the kids," Hein said. "In high school it's a 12-inch ball." Living in California, she plays ball year-round. When she lived in the Northeast for a short time, Hein was dismayed to find she could play only in the summer.

As a child growing up in California, Hein played softball with the Girls' Athletic Association, an after-school recreational league, because schools did not have girls' teams. After school there was no place else to go. Because Hein remained single until she was 52, she played for many years. "I could do what I wanted," she said. She married for the first time after what her husband described as "a whirlwind courtship of 10 and a half years." Hein said her husband "didn't enjoy the game much for a number of years but has become an exceptional fan."

A retired secretary at Hughes Aircraft, Hein said, "Looking back, I believe team sports and the cooperation with others that is necessary aids in working with others in business to a common goal." Hein likes belonging to a team with a common goal, a bond. "We sometimes have birthday celebrations, yard sales, or meet just to visit or help someone with a project or problem," she said.

"Mostly I love playing. It has been an integral part of my life for the past 30 years. I am a competitor, and that includes competing with myself—being better today than yesterday—and there is fun in that. The camaraderie and friendships made are a large part of the team effort—10 or 11 people doing their best to help achieve their best effort. Win or lose, if you've done the best you could, the outcome cannot lessen your effort.

"I am probably driven partially by the fact that I have some skill at the game," Hein said, "and that has some bearing on how much you enjoy something. A side benefit is a continued feeling of youth."

~

Softball has always been more available to girls, at least informally, than most other team sports. It was something you could play in the backyard or at a picnic with whoever was around without raising too much protest from the gender police. Many of the women in this book played softball as kids, usually with their brothers and their friends, and it wasn't until Little League tryouts that the stress began—when girls were told they could not play.

"I learned to use both hands because I had to use my brother's left-handed mitt," said Linda Van Valkenberg, 51, a physical education teacher from the Bronx, New York. "I was always a better player than my brother," she quipped, "and he resented it." Van Valkenberg went to a Little League tryout, and they thought she was a boy because she had her hair up under her ball cap. When they said she passed, Van Valkenberg took off her cap to sign up, and she was told, "Oh, you can't join."

Van Valkenberg said her dad taught her older brother how to play ball, and she watched. Because there were no baseball teams for girls in school, she played with her brother's friends and also with school clubs.

Then there's the other side of the coin—a legend about Dot Richardson, shortstop on the 1996 and 2000 Olympic gold medal United States Women's Softball Teams. As a child, Richardson was invited by a Little League coach to join his team if she would promise to pretend to be a boy. She turned him down.

Softball is available to women as they grow up. Neighborhood mixed teams exist all over the country, and many companies have softball teams, either mixed or single sex. Many bars and social clubs sponsor teams.

But softball is not hardball either figuratively or literally. It began as an indoor version of baseball and was always considered a "soft" sport, which is why it was not taken as seriously as Major League Baseball, for example. It has been called "sissy ball," "kitten ball," "ladies baseball," and "mush ball." In fact, the head of the Amateur Softball Association (ASA) dubbed softball "the girl's national game" in a 1939 article in *Look* magazine after he realized that more women were playing softball than any other sport. This compelled the ASA to add this warning to their rule book in 1940:

"It is the consensus of the ASA commissioners that, for health's sake, girls should not engage in more than three softball games in any one week, and that girls under the age of 15 years should not be used in any major softball competition."

Women continued to ignore the rules and play softball. Some of the best places for women to play competitive softball were the industrial leagues—most sponsored by forward-thinking companies for their employees—and pro leagues of the 1960s and '70s. These leagues became the training ground for athletes like Dot Richardson. Probably the most influential industrial league team was sponsored by a brake lining company in Stratford, Connecticut, called the Raybestos Brakettes. In 1965 the Brakettes, often called the New York Yankees of women's softball, launched a world tour to promote women's softball and won 21 national championships.

Their best-known pitcher, Joan Joyce, dubbed a female Babe Ruth, had a fastball that was once clocked at 116 miles an hour. In her early years she had a hard time controlling it. Legend has it that a workman on top of a telephone pole saw her pitching and came down later to give her some tips. A softball pitcher himself, he told her to use a slingshot motion instead of a windmill motion. It worked, and she went on to 6,648 strikeouts in 3,972 innings. Joyce competed with baseball legend Ted Williams in an exhibition before a crowd of nearly 20,000 people in Waterbury, Connecticut. Some of Joyce's 40 pitches were in excess of 100 miles an hour, and Williams could get only one base hit and one foul hit.

Joyce was one of the founders in 1976 of the International Women's Professional Softball Association that played for four seasons before folding for lack of funds.

~

Sue Nesbihal, a 51-year-old probation officer on Long Island, New York, remembers her 10 years of playing industrial softball as some of the best ball she ever played, especially one fabulous triple play. She remembers how she felt, if not all of the details of the play. Nesbihal was a left-handed catcher, and her friend Jean was the pitcher.

"We were a dynamite duo," she said. "I was running and running, and I just stuck my glove out, and the ball was in my glove." The rest of the players were flabbergasted, according to Nesbihal. "Nobody would believe it. Everyone thought the batter got home. I felt like a big leaguer," she said. "That was the only reward. And the fun of going out for a beer after the game."

Nesbihal worked for the Nassau County Department of Social Services, and their team played against Grummond, Avis, Pan Am, and other Long Island industries, who all had better uniforms, according to Nesbihal.

"Pan Am players had sky blue shorts, a white shirt with lettering, and kneesocks." She said her County DSS team was a ragtag team, although they were Division A. At first they had uniforms, but they were "made of that horrible fabric that makes you sweat more." Nesbihal said they eventually had T-shirts and shorts. "You could tell the haves from the have-nots," she quipped. She often wished she worked for Pan Am because they used to fly their players to out-of-town games. Grummond had their own field. Nevertheless, Nesbihal played high-caliber softball for 10 years and always made the play-offs.

Nesbihal's father, Mike Garofola, was a Little League coach and so let her play in the boys' games when she was a child. He knew the 12-year-old boys were not as good as his 10-year-old daughter, who could already throw a softball 240 feet. Nesbihal played one-on-one with her brother, who is now a head coach at the State University of New York at Stony Brook.

"My dad told me he had a cup of coffee with the New York Giants during the war years. I don't know if he ever got into a game, but he was a first baseman for them for a while. His best man at his wedding was a pitcher with the Giants who had the record for walking the most batters in a row." Nesbihal said her dad "wanted a boy for his first child, but he got a girl and so decided that his daughter would just have to be the athlete." Her parents came to all the award dinners and games (they sat through a doubleheader) and were supportive. Her mom didn't get it, Nesbihal said, but "she knew I had a talent."

Nesbihal said there was no program for girls in elementary school, but her friends formed a team and "we would walk from one school to the other, as much as two miles." This seemed a longer way because they were little kids.

"I ran in the Long Island Marathon the other day," she said, "and passed that school. It certainly brought back some memories."

Nesbihal credits her skill to having her dad teach her at a young age. "There are certain things you learn when you're young," she said, "like knowing the break on a ball, observing the unconscious body language of players." Little girls playing since they were four understand this. In high school, Nesbihal had offers of athletic scholarships, but in those days, just as Title IX was becoming law, "you had to play 19 sports." There was no scholarship for girls for one sport. After college she had a chance to play in a pro league for $25 a game.

Nesbihal stopped playing softball at 45 only because she lost her depth perception and missed a fly ball. Rather than do that again, she switched to track and field, and now at the Empire State Senior

Games she competes in running, discus, and javelin. She has won three gold medals and set the record for the 2000-meter steeplechase. She said doing 26 laps on a track takes mental toughness. It's different than running along a road.

"I'm not that fast," she said. "I'm like the Energizer Bunny. I just keep going and going and going."

~

For a couple of years in the 1970s, Patricia Klammer left her Long Island teaching job every Friday and drove two and a half hours to spend the weekend in Reading, Pennsylvania, training for games with her professional fast-pitch softball league. For this, she earned $100 a week as a member of the Pennsylvania Liberties. Klammer, now 55, a physical education teacher in a Seaford junior high school, said there were eight or ten teams, and she also played with a team in Buffalo, New York, for a while.

The game schedule was mostly from June to August, but Klammer said during this time the women's leagues were starting to draw audiences. Klammer was an infielder, but she has played all positions. She said there were some really great players including Diane Killiam and Donna Lopiano, now executive director of the Women's Sports Foundation.

Klammer continues to play on local teams. "I have been playing softball for 35 years on various fast- and slow-pitch teams." Because most teams play only about 10 times each season, Klammer finds it necessary to belong to more than one team. She said playing is so much a part of her that each time she tries to give it up, she fails. Last time, someone called her and said they needed players 50 and over for a senior team, and she got involved again. Klammer went to Tallahassee, Florida, for the 50-plus Senior Games tournament and said she was impressed with how many women were playing. "There were 375 women there," she said. "Each year, more and more women are playing."

Linda Van Valkenberg said, "I felt my career in sports was winding down until I discovered the Senior Games two years ago. Now my whole outlook has brightened, and I have something to look forward to for the rest of my life." Through a friend she got involved in the Senior Games and came in second in the discus throw.

"I never did it before," she said, "but a friend told me if you can throw a ball you can do this, so I tried." Van Valkenberg, who coached high school sports most of her life, organized a softball team for the Senior Games of 2000, and she plays with the Silver Edge, a bar league in her neighborhood with a team of women between 20 and 57. How has her playing changed over the years? "I gave up sliding 10 years ago, and I prefer to avoid collisions with other players," Van Valkenberg said.

Klammer, who teaches physical education, believes playing team sports "absolutely strengthens one's feeling of self-worth, confidence, and group belonging. It prepares women for an active, aggressive role in work and life." However, she believes that today—since Title IX— the competition for athletic scholarships is so fierce that girls need to go to the sports camps for intense training.

When Klammer was a child, there were no scholarships for women. She played on a boys' Little League team for one year when she was 9 or 10. In college she played basketball, and for a while after graduation she played that sport with Amateur Athletic Union teams.

~

Sylvia "Tommy" Thomas, of Beaver Falls, Pennsylvania, played softball for 65 years. She stopped at 80 when she had a mild heart attack.

Now she goes bowling with a league. Thomas began playing softball when she was 15, mostly with boys.

In 1994, Barbara "Raisin" Racine, 66, of Oakland, California, organized the Silver Streaks, a softball team for women over 60. Racine, who had always played team sports, retired from the military when she was 55 and went in search of a game. She didn't find any right away, but she kept looking. Finally, she found some players from Colorado and joined them. She played with many other teams from other states, but she wanted to have a game closer to home. Besides, she was tired of practicing by herself. Racine told a *Real Sports* reporter, "I would drive around to ballparks and I would see a gray-haired woman and ask, 'How old are you?' If she was over 55, I'd say, 'you're mine.'" Persistence paid off for Racine, and the Silver Streaks became reality; she even convinced Reebok to provide uniforms and warm-ups. Since the Silver Streaks began in 1994, the number of senior women's softball teams in the San Francisco Bay Area has grown.

"I've been pitching for 40 years," said Norma Franzese, 65, of Mesa, Arizona, whose team, the Queen Bees, won the gold at the Senior Games four years in a row. "We won the National Senior World Series in Phoenix in October 1999."

Franzese, who played sports with boys in childhood, organized the Queen Bees in 1994, after her retirement, and they play six or seven days a week against other women's or men's teams. "We play the men 69 and 70," she said. "We only have four players under 60; four are 65, and one is 70. We play the 55-plus with women."

PLAYING HARDBALL

It wasn't until the 1996 Olympics (the non–Senior Olympics) when the American women won the gold for softball—in its first year as an Olympic event—that anybody took the sport seriously. Before they knew it might be popular, TV producers decided such a game would be of little interest to general viewers, so they did not air it, and nobody got to see it.

Now that women's softball has been accepted, many women are trying to bring that same acceptance to women's baseball. The lingering image of softball as a sissy game fuels the formation of a baseball league for women. The Women's National Adult Baseball Association in San Diego reports 85 teams in 20 cities in the United States.

"We play hardball!" This proclamation is from the New York/ New Jersey Regional Women's Baseball League established for women 18 and up "to give them the opportunity to compete in a sport that many grew up playing, yet were inadvertently thwarted from pursuing into adulthood. Finally," they say, "here's your chance to try the alternative to softball."

It wasn't until the 1992 movie *A League of Their Own* prompted the press to increase its coverage of women's baseball that women turned out in great numbers for tryouts. The movie was an eye-opener for women who never knew that women's baseball existed. Although male promoters were behind the organization of women's baseball in the 1940s and thought they would make money by having the women wear short skirts, the players rallied at the chance to play, whatever the reason. The league actually played a combination of baseball and softball. Recently, these wartime athletes were immortalized in an exhibition at the National Baseball Hall of Fame and Museum in Cooperstown, New York.

Richard Hopkins, the manager of the Arizona Cactus Wrens, a women's baseball team, believes women's baseball is set to take off as the next big sport. Australia has more than 60 women's teams that play. England has women that play alongside the men. Unlike women's basketball, which has the support of the NBA, Major League Baseball has refused to acknowledge women's baseball. Hopkins said one of his players "pitches more than 80 miles per hour and hits 350-foot home runs."

The Women's Sports Foundation commissioned a study called "Women and Baseball: Psychological and Sociological Aspects of Women's Participation in Men's Professional Baseball." This was meant to answer the question: "Can the best women compete in men's professional baseball?" The study found that body mass and strength were less important than experience and skill. "Baseball is a game of skills that are combinations of timing, coordination, strength, knowledge of the game, strategies, control, and savvy." They cited several examples of smaller male players who were amazing players.

The study concluded that the biggest disadvantage that women players will have to overcome will be their inexperience in playing baseball. Even though baseball and softball are similar games, subtle differences such as the smaller size and weight of the ball, the longer pitching distances and base paths, and the larger field size will pose more disadvantages than differences in physical size or ability. Women players will need time to adjust to this new game. Their relative success—or lack of it—in the first season of such an endeavor, given that most women do not have the extensive baseball background of Little League through the minors that the men have, should not be taken as an indication of the absolute potential that women have to play baseball.

Most softball skills will directly transfer to baseball. Women already throw overhand in all positions other than pitcher in softball, for example. Throwing underhand involves the same principles and skills of throwing overhand, so acquisition of overhand pitching techniques will not be difficult. Women will just need time to develop overhand pitches because of their lack of experience with the specific skill.

~

Whether they play softball or baseball, women continue to get short shrift. Recently, while reading a story in the Long Island daily, *Newsday*, about a high school softball player, Sue Nesbihal found herself getting angry.

"Nothing has changed," she said about an article about Breanne Nasti, a 17-year-old who plays center field for Baldwin High School. The gist of the article was that the girl was being misunderstood because she was so good. Meanwhile, Nasti has been named the best player on Long Island, she has a .769 season batting average, a .656 career average, has set national records, and was named center fielder of the decade by the New York State Sportswriters and Coaches Association for Girls' Sports.

"She has been accused of being a showboat, of showing off," Nesbihal said. Nasti has been criticized because she bunted to fool the other team, which had played deep because Nasti is known to hit long drives to the outfield.

"They wouldn't say that about a boy," Nesbihal said. She's right. It wouldn't even have been a story.

PART II

Sexual Politics:
Men vs. Women with Balls

7

DADDY'S GIRLS

~

"I originally thought that we would be appealing more to the proverbial soccer moms, but I soon realized that the real appeal of the Women's World Cup in the United States is to those soccer dads out there who are looking to connect with their daughters. And this is the perfect opportunity for them."

—Jack Bell, "Sign Off" column, TV Guide, June 1999

In a junior high school gym in South Brooklyn, New York, on a Sunday afternoon a handful of people, mostly dads, watched two teams of teenaged girls play basketball in the New York Police Department 78th precinct recreational league. The players wore red or yellow jumpers over their regular clothes. The red team coach paced the sidelines and occasionally said "damn" after a failed play. The referee warned him on it. The other coach, also a man, also paced, but he was the silent type.

"You want a Gatorade?" a dad asked his daughter during a time-out. "I have it in the car." She had said no to this question earlier, but then seemed to realize her dad wanted to do this. This tall, good-looking man wearing a gray sweatshirt with a corporate logo got up eagerly when his daughter said yes. He left the gym and came back in a few minutes. He cheered for his daughter with great pride, although, like most of the others, he cheered for a good play by either team. That was a noticeable thing here.

Throughout the game, when any of the players did well or simply made a nice effort, the response came from everyone in the crowd, regardless of which team they were there to see. For example, during the second half of the game, a yellow team player, a small girl with speed like a bullet, used her body to effectively block anyone who came at her. It was almost like watching a football player. She rose from the floor and twisted in the air so her back was like a wedge clearing the path for others. All of the fathers in the audience were highly impressed.

Whenever there was a time-out, one or another parent went out to get a drink or snack for a daughter. They always asked the referee, a husky young man with a fashionably thin line of beard traveling around his jaw, if they could bring him something—water, Gatorade, a soda. He always said, "Oh, thanks. Wait, I'll get my wallet." Invariably, they said, "Don't worry about it." This little ceremony apparently continued throughout the day, for the same man refereed most games and was obviously appreciated by fathers interested in keeping him happy.

At halftime another father walked out onto the court. He found his daughter and put his arm around her shoulder, congratulating her on her good game. The he proudly stood by while she practiced some layups. During the last quarter, the wife and two younger children of the man in the sweatshirt came into the gym and joined him.

A basket by the yellow team at the final buzzer brought great cheers from this small crowd. The player who scored the winning basket had hurt her ankle earlier in the game, but she had refused to be benched.

MY DAUGHTER THE ATHLETE

Fathers have always known something that most moms did not—that playing at team sports is fun, and it makes you feel good. It's obvious that men have a large interest in and influence on today's athletic women. Sports have always been a guy thing. Fathers have always taught their sons how to play catch, join the Little League, and follow the manly path of athletics. However, many fathers of women in this book did the same for their daughters before it was politically correct. Today's daddy's girls are not spoiled darlings. They are athletes.

When Title IX gave girls a greater opportunity to play team sports, it opened up new opportunities for men, too. They were right there to see that their daughters played all the sports they could. Today's dads are having more fun than earlier ones who had to fight to get their daughters into Little League and those who knew whatever team sports they played would not be available for the girls when they became women.

When school team sports became open to girls, fathers began coaching their daughters and encouraging them to apply for athletic scholarships. While mothers also provided encouragement, with few exceptions, most had little experience with sports themselves. They didn't really get it and might bring their sewing or a book to read or they might chat with friends while they sat in the bleachers. A few moms discouraged their daughters by refusing to drive them to practice, or warned them they would get hurt and told them that playing was not ladylike. The woman who joined her husband for the 78th precinct game had come to meet the family, but she showed no real interest in the game.

According to a Chilton Sports Poll in 1999, men like women's sports more than women do: 44 percent of men vs. 38 percent of women like to watch the WNBA, and 34 percent of men vs. 25 percent of women like to watch women's college basketball. This may explain why more men than women were in the bleachers at that school in South Brooklyn.

But having those parents—dads and moms—encourage their daughters means a lot. According to a study by the Melpomene Institute in St. Paul, Minnesota, girls who are encouraged in sports by their fathers are less likely to date abusive men. The study of 865 girls aged 7 to 17 revealed that fathers are most likely to support their daughters' activity by teaching them skills, coaching, and playing and practicing with them; mothers are most likely to support them with positive feedback and by coming to games.

Zan Taylor, who coaches the 78th precinct girls basketball teams, was herself a daddy's girl.

Taylor's dad fought for her right to play sports. "He went to the Little League meetings," she said, "to push the issue. They would say, 'OK, she can play, but she can't pitch.' Or else they would say I could only play certain positions."

"But I had to play," she said, after her dad went through all that. Taylor has coached and played women's basketball for most of her life. She coached women's college basketball for 10 years at Columbia University, Long Island University, and State University of New York at Old Westbury. She is a New Yorker who lived for the first few years of her childhood in South Carolina. Her dad used to coach the high school boys, and he encouraged her in sports. The second oldest of seven kids (five girls, two boys), Taylor said she was "a daddy's girl." Her mom had played basketball in high school but did not continue.

About her late father, soccer player Mary McNichol said, "He loved having five girls." McNichol said her father was raised by a single mom who believed in women's equality, and he had the attitude that his daughters could do whatever they wanted. "He was always coaching us," McNichol recalled. "He took us to golf outings, wrestling matches, baseball games. We had a basketball hoop in the backyard. We went as a family to all the Princeton games (his alma mater) and all the sports events in Philadelphia. He told us, 'No daughter of mine is going to be a cheerleader—cheering on the men.'" So, with this strong encouragement, his daughters played various team sports all their lives. McNichol and her sister Antoinette, who is just two years older, often played on the same school teams.

"I remember our team would go into a huddle with the coach, and then at halftime my dad would call us over and the others would follow us. He'd give us some more advice on strategy. He came to every game we played," McNichol said.

Mary McNichol was bigger and more aggressive than her sister Antoinette, but Antoinette had better skills. Their father never pointed that out. McNichol said her father was not a physically demonstrative person, even though all the girls knew he loved them. "But one day he told me, 'When I see you on the basketball court, you are so graceful, you're like a ballet dancer.'"

It wasn't until McNichol got to college that she found out that playing sports was not the coolest thing for a woman to do. Her father died when she was 19 and in her sophomore year at college. Ironically, the following year she dropped out of sports. "I hated the coach," she said.

Wanda Blailock and Nikki Leader, who now play basketball with the Louisiana Tigerettes Hi-Tops, said their father was their biggest inspiration. He taught his three daughters to enjoy sports and never missed one of their games at school. Wanda recalled that their younger brother played sports, too, but was not as enamored of their father's "coaching."

"My brother walked off the court" after their father yelled at him about a play, Blailock said. She laughed at the recollection. "We were used to that, but he wasn't."

Alexandria rower Rhonda Taylor said, "Any sport that my sister and I wanted to get involved in, my dad was all for it. I ran track from the 5th to the 12th grade. Every Saturday morning or any time I had a track meet, he and my mom would get up early and prepare all the fixin's for that day's events." Taylor said while her mom packed the beverages and snacks, she and her dad "would make sure my spikes and other track gear was ready to go. Then he and I would go to the track meets, and he would sit in the stands all day cheering me and my teammates on, comforting me, and just being there as a source of support. Whenever there were organizational meetings or a need for parent participation, he was always there. I also played basketball, and he was there for those games as well. I remember once when a ref called a bad foul at a game, he (my dad) jumped up and told the ref he was wrong. It caused my coach to get a technical foul. I was horrified at the time but look back on the moment with fondness," Taylor said.

SOME MIXED MESSAGES

Many women got their start in sports and sports careers because of their coaching dads, but at the same time, some got mixed messages from from their fathers.

"It was more of a way to do something with him," Patty Jayne of Portland, Oregon, said. Jayne, who is a volleyball player and coach, said her father coached her brothers' teams, so he had access to the school gym. Jayne is the seventh of eight children.

"We used to pester him to take us to the gym on Sunday mornings." He would open up the gym, according to Jayne, "but this was no picnic. We had ball-handling drills. He wouldn't just let us play. He told us you can't play without the fundamentals." In the late 1970s Jayne wanted to play softball, but her dad told her she couldn't because she'd get hurt.

"It confused me," Jayne said. "I was too young to understand. I still carry it with me. That's one of my [hot] buttons."

Joy McCarthy, a corporate psychologist in Atlanta, Georgia, got a mixed message, too. McCarthy, now 57, was offered a chance to play semipro basketball after college in 1960, but her father, who had coached and encouraged her athletic career throughout her childhood and through college, then said, "Absolutely not." McCarthy was devastated. There were six kids in McCarthy's family, three of each sex. McCarthy's father was the basketball coach for their church team of seventh and eighth graders.

McCarthy made the team in sixth grade, but her father would not let her play until the pastor told him it was OK to put her in the game. McCarthy already loved sports and went to a private girls school "where it was good to be athletic." Her dad "was a tremendous supporter. He'd go over strategy, tell me the patterns. These are some of my favorite memories."

Once she was in college, McCarthy realized, it was no longer OK to be an athlete. She admitted not knowing how she really felt about these mixed messages. Her dad actually began to teach her how to lose. She said, in the bowling league, "he'd say, 'Now, Joy, you have to throw gutter balls. Men don't like girls that beat 'em.'"

Years later, McCarthy realized that her father was only trying to do what he thought was best for her. "He didn't want me to be unhappy. He thought making a husband happy was probably more important in the long run than a career in basketball."

When she became a suburban housewife she played tennis, but when she beat her husband, they stopped playing. When she was in a tournament, she said, her husband wouldn't come to watch her play. In the world that existed then, it would have been tough for her to be a professional athlete. But McCarthy's athletic spirit didn't just curl up and die. She puts her sports background to good use as a corporate psychologist who helps women understand the rules of the game.

FATHERS AS ADVOCATES

"The sport feminism of dads with athletic daughters has inexorably changed the nature of the battle for sports resources," claims the Women's Sports Foundation. This power struggle is less gender-based than age-based, with athletic directors, school principals, college presidents, and other decision makers who grew up in a culture that taught them that women are not interested in sports (or should not be), girls can't throw, no one will pay to see women, etc. As members of this "dinosaur" generation retire and dads and moms with athletic daughters assume the reins of power in sports, the dynamics of the gender equity struggle will change dramatically.

One of this new generation is Kevin O'Neill, superintendent of the Coopersville public schools in Michigan, who has been pushing for gender equity in sports not only for his two daughters, but for everyone. He was profiled in *Gball*, the girl's basketball magazine sponsored by the women's basketball division of the Amateur Athletic Union. According to *Gball*, O'Neill led the way in rebuilding a tiny girls' locker room and passing a bond to renovate a high school, with the aim of creating equal facilities. He said, however, facilities are easy to change, "the harder thing is the attitudes." O'Neill said that at every sporting event, he and others in his school district go to the opponents' bleachers and talk to parents from other schools. He asks them what recognition girls' sports get in those schools.

With these small questions, he wants to get them thinking. His administration also gives free tickets to the girls' high school games to the elementary students, so they can come and be part of the excitement.

Bill Kennedy, a real estate and construction entrepreneur of Chicago, actually started a professional women's volleyball league because he was so inspired by what the sport did for his daughter's self-esteem.

Don Sabo, a professor of sociology at D'Youville College in Buffalo, New York, a trustee of the Women's Sports Foundation, and a former NCAA Division I defensive football player and captain, is a leader in helping women succeed in team sports and in educating men about the inequities. He has given many examples of how dads are demanding equality for their daughters.

One of Sabo's examples is about a mortgage loan officer and volunteer basketball coach from Dallas, Texas, who, when he first saw his nine-year-old daughter's gym, was shocked by the poor conditions. There were no bleachers—just a worn linoleum tile floor and incandescent lighting. The boys' gym, in contrast, was modern and well equipped. This father joined forces with other parents to bring media attention to the inequities, and he helped to educate the school board on matters pertaining to Title IX.

At leadership conferences Sabo helps dispel the myths that men have created about women athletes. In 1994 at a JCPenney Women's Sports Leadership Conference attended by high school athletes on Long Island, New York, he found that once boys stopped to think about it, they changed their minds about all the stereotypes about women in sports.

In writing about men discovering Title IX, Sabo said, "I was impressed by the boys' general receptivity to the message and morality of Title IX." In the early 1980s, few men were fighting for gender equity in sports. Sabo believes that today more men are waking up to the fact that gender equity is their issue as well as women's.

This new generation of men with athletic daughters will demonstrate that pride in the abilities of their children is more important than support of male dominance in sports, according to the Women's Sports Foundation, but there is no reason to think it will happen globally.

8

THE CUTTING EDGE OF COACHING

~

*" 'The girls are fun to coach,' Coach Conte would say. 'Boys are often
sometimes there just for the ride. Girls, they tend to appreciate it more.'
'They listen,' Coach Moyer would reply. 'Boys, you have to tear down
their ego. With girls, you just have to build up their confidence.' "*

—Dialogue of two male coaches from
In These Girls, Hope Is a Muscle, by Madeleine Blais

COACHING FEMALE ATHLETES drums up arguments no matter whom you talk to. Women athletes respond differently to male and female coaches, some say. Or do they? Women coaches don't see eye to eye on how best to create a winning team of women. Male coaches don't see why their tried-and-true techniques don't work with women as they do with men, while others insist they do work.

There are many assumptions about coaching women. People of both sexes will say that if you want the team to win, you need a male coach because men have experience and know-how. But then, how do you explain Pat Summitt and her winning record coaching women's basketball at the University of Tennessee? On the other hand, how come many of the women coaches of the WNBA teams have been replaced by men?

Women coaches have learned their trade from men, and when they use the same aggressive and boisterous style of coaching, it doesn't always work on women players. Division I volleyball coach Patty Jayne of Portland, Oregon, got so burned out with coaching the women's team at the University of Portland after five years that she took a year off to "gain some perspective."

"If I've only been coached by men, how do I know any different?" said Jayne, who had only one woman coach in her entire career in school. She pointed out that the early women's coaches had no experience as players. Most were gym teachers. A championship athlete who went to college on scholarships, Jayne is driven and intense, like the men she learned coaching from, including her father, who coached CYO (Catholic Youth Organization) basketball teams in the 1970s. Jayne discovered, however, that her style and intensity didn't translate when coaching women. "Girls tolerate a lot more from a man," Jayne said.

Sports psychologist Carole Oglesby tends to agree. "Women accept [a screaming style] from a male coach, but most definitely will not accept it from a woman coach," Oglesby said. She said she finds this very distressing. "Girls think the man is a better coach, even if he has equal talent with a female coach. This is just the norm we've been led to believe," said Oglesby, who is a physical education professor at Temple University in Philadelphia, Pennsylvania, and president of WomenSport International. Oglesby said that if a coach is mean, the girl often blames herself.

Kim Oden, assistant coach for varsity women's volleyball at Stanford University and a former Olympian, agrees that women who have been coached by men are pretty intense. She finds this frustrating because, she said, "Girls these days expect something maternal, something soft from a coach. The females in their lives have been like that. They bake cookies, make dinner. In Division I, I don't want to be a nurturer. You have to be a leader, a disciplinarian."

Stefanie Pemper, head women's basketball coach at Bowdoin College in Maine, considers herself more of an educator. She agreed that the coaching issue is misunderstood and said there's lots of bad information out there at the high school and the college level.

"I found the winningest teams are often coached by men (in general) who have a pressing style, are very aggressive," she said, referring to the yellers and screamers. "I provide my women with more support, more understanding. I find out what they enjoy and try to motivate them. I want to know how to connect, communicate.

"I don't think they need to learn by failure," Pemper said. "It's such a critical thing. I feel very good when I go home after I've had a good conversation with a player." Women often respond to conversation. Yet Pemper admitted, "I struggle with not wanting to pay too much attention, or do too much hand holding. If a player needs to figure it out, then she'll figure it out." She said some players think she's mad at them if she doesn't want to have a conversation.

Pemper spoke of a male coach of a women's team who is well liked and very successful. "He said he doesn't have a team meeting. When he asks the team what the two players who requested a meeting had in mind, they tell him they have no idea. He says, 'exactly.' "

April Heinrichs, who succeeded Tony DiCicco as coach of the U.S. Women's National Soccer Team, let the team know right away that she cared more about winning than worrying about their feelings.

Judy Love, volleyball coach at Western Oregon High School, told sportswriter Greg Jayne of the *Statesman Journal* in Salem, Oregon, (and husband of coach Patty Jayne), "The way women work out problems is much different from the way men work out problems.

They want to process it and talk it out, while guys might go slam their fist against the locker."

YELLERS AND SCREAMERS BEWARE

Tony DiCicco, former coach of the Women's National Soccer Team, was raised by an athletic mother and appears not to have developed the stereotypical biases against women. He told sportswriter Jere Longman that women want to be challenged, but they don't want a coach screaming in their faces. In fact, according to Longman, a comment made by a member of DiCicco's team, Mia Hamm, "Coach us like men, treat us like women," inspired the heading of a chapter in his book, *The Girls of Summer: The U.S. Women's Soccer Team and How It Changed the World*.

One of the male coaches of the women's hockey organization the Chicago Ice learned the hard way that screamers weren't appreciated when the women voted him out of a job.

Mike Walsh, who coaches a New Jersey girls' high school lacrosse team, tells of having spoken sternly to the girls one day. He said they didn't speak to him for days and let him know never to do that again. This coach thinks boys might be more used to stern talk. Nevertheless, when he was named coach of the year by a New Jersey newspaper, an article reported that all the girls said they liked that he showed respect for them by not yelling.

Women definitely resist being yelled at, and Womanship, an Annapolis, Maryland, sailing school by and for women, bases its teaching program on the premise, "nobody yells." An article in *Sail* magazine by Suzanne Pogell and Andrea Sachs reported, "Almost two-thirds of the respondents were attracted to Womanship because of its 'nobody yells' policy. Harsh tones and words often slip out when sailing because of the need to react swiftly, move quickly, and not dawdle over one maneuver. However, in a learning environment, yelling is detrimental and regressive. Women are quick to point out that yelling erodes confidence, intimidates, and shuts down the learning process."

According to Womanship, "Yelling also sets up a kind of hierarchy, giving one person all the authority and control." A survey of 940 women sponsored by *Sail* magazine and Womanship in the spring of 1996 found that, "Teams are most productive and successful when the playing field is level, when all members work together, and when the instructor counsels and suggests, but does not reign. Learning takes place and confidence builds in an atmosphere where questions, answers, and suggestions can flow freely."

CAN WOMEN TAKE CRITICISM?

"Women internalize everything," DiCicco told Longman. "You get them in a room together and you say, 'We have a few players who are not fit' and they all think you are talking about them. Say the same thing to the guys and they go, 'Yeah, coach is right, I'm the only fit one. Everyone else is dogging it.'"

"The main difference between girls and boys," said Linda Van Valkenberg, a public school coach who has coached boys as well as girls, "is that the girls are very temperamental. Because of this you have to be very careful how you speak to them. Otherwise they take what you say personally and feel hurt and sulk. Then their playing suffers. Boys, on the other hand, know that you're talking about their playing and not them personally. They realize that you are trying to improve their skills. With a little encouragement, they just try harder. Boys you can tell what to do and they do it. You have to ask the girls, and sometimes if they don't like the way you ask, they are very slow to respond."

Soccer player Mary Ellen Mellor, a varsity girls' coach at Archbishop Carroll High School in Radnor, Pennsylvania, said, "Girls are harder to motivate, but better team players." Boys just do it. "If girls have a complaint, it's all over the place in a minute. Boys just grumble but don't complain."

In her book *How Men Think*, gender psychologist Adrienne Mendell wrote, "Women talk to other women about their feelings. Chances are if I upset a woman, my secretary will come in and ask, 'Why did you treat her that way?' With a man, chances are 99.9 percent that no one else will know if he is upset. He wouldn't want anyone to know if he is upset. He wouldn't want anyone to know he was criticized."

Mendell wrote about her early sailing racing team experience, "I learned about taking criticism while sailing with Rex, a well-liked and highly respected skipper. As a novice racer, I asked Rex for a crew position on his boat. I expected him to ask about my sailing ability. Instead he responded, 'Can you take abuse?' I thought he was joking, but I soon learned otherwise."

TOO MUCH POWER AND CONTROL

Throughout sports history some male coaches of men's teams have been notorious for abusing their power. For example, in the spring of 2000, Bobby Knight, the longtime coach of the Indiana University men's basketball team, received only a slap on the wrist for years of incidents of bad behavior, including choking a player and throwing an object at a female office worker, to mention just a few. Public outrage and newspaper editorials finally forced the university administration to fire Knight in mid-2000.

This kind of abuse of power with women can quickly translate to sexual harassment and abuse. When she was 14, Zan Taylor went to play basketball with Brooklyn USA. This was her first experience with women's basketball and one she will never forget.

"You gotta get these layups," a coach yelled at a player, and then the coach proceeded to "smack her in the face." When Taylor saw that, she packed up her sports bag and walked out. "No way was I going to play for him."

Women and girls are more frequent victims of harassment and abuse than men and boys, and many females drop out of sports rather than continue to be subjected to the undermining effects of constant mistreatment. Others endure the sexual attention of their male coaches or peers because of fear, desire for athletic reward, low self-esteem, or ignorance of who to turn to for help. Typically, abused athletes in high school or college keep quiet because they fear that they will be accused of consenting or of inventing the whole thing. They are also afraid of retaliation by the coach, having playing time reduced, or losing a scholarship. Our society wants girls and women to have self-esteem, but the system often treats them like victims or liars if they speak up about harassment.

Sports psychologist Carole Oglesby, who does sexual harassment training, finds that sexual abuse is becoming much more prevalent in sports. "I did a very informal survey [on college teams]," she said. She asked two questions: First, do you know anyone on a team who dated a coach or had sex with a coach? Second, did it make a difference to the team? She said that everybody questioned answered "Oh, yeah" to the first question. To the second question they said, "It really messed up the team."

Oglesby's organization WomenSport International and other groups say romance and sex between coaches and players is an abuse of power that undermines the mission of athletics.

Consensual dating and power is another aspect of the issue. Rick Tekip, 31, met his girlfriend Jen Stitzell because she was a player on a Chicago Ice hockey team he joined as an assistant coach. Tekip admitted this could have made the relationship and his job difficult, so he quit coaching Stitzell's squad and just comes to see her play.

While there is no long-term research on harassment of women in sports, recent studies, including those by WomenSport International, indicate that sexual harassment and abuse is just as much a problem in sports as it is elsewhere in society. Many sports organizations do not have adequate mechanisms in place to help protect frightened athletes and to exclude harassers and abusers. Both the Women's Sports Foundation and WomenSport International publish brochures to help players and coaches understand what sexual harassment is.

As more women play team sports that are coached by men, complaints of abuse and sexual harassment will likely become just as common as they are in business, politics, and the military—any area women are entering.

MEN WHO LOVE COACHING WOMEN

"NBA Coach Finds Joy in Women's League" was the headline over a *New York Times* story about Richie Adubato, coach of the WNBA New York Liberty. After 40 years of coaching men, Adubato's life has turned around, and he appears to love it, although he admitted he is sometimes baffled by the women who cry if they win and cry if they lose.

Carol Blazejowski, Liberty general manager, was skeptical about hiring a man who had never coached women before. But he loves basketball and is not a screamer.

Other men, including Van Chancellor, coach of the WNBA Houston Comets; Geno Auriemma, coach of the University of Connecticut women's basketball team; and Tony DiCicco, have made names for themselves and their teams by coaching women and seem to enjoy their roles as pioneers. And they have done so with style and dignity. There may be a certain amount of pride in being on the front lines of this new arena of women's sports, and also in the experience of coaching women, who do respond differently than men.

Marcy Bright, who plays hockey with the Chicago Ice, believes the enthusiasm of their male coaches may stem from never having had daughters to coach. Two coaches, who each have two sons who also play hockey, bring their sons to the games. "They never had the joy of coaching a daughter. Maybe that's why they coach us." The Chicago Ice has several coaches, all men, and they represent the wide range of personality styles, current attitudes, and arguments in coaching women.

Bright, who has been playing with the Ice since 1996, described her coaches as "the keys to my success as a hockey player." She feels this way even about Larry Wisniewski, the coach who was voted out because of his screaming. She describes him as a "finesse" player who teaches his students to "dance" with the puck around defenders by using innovative skills and creativity. He also became the coach of Bright's squad in her first season with the Chicago Ice.

"Larry was a screamer. He was a very intense coach who expected a lot from his players. He did not see us as women. He saw us as hockey players," said Bright. "I remember skating around on eggshells, praying not to make a mistake or do something that would make him mad. I realize today that the reason he yelled at me was because he could see my future as a player, and he wanted to push me harder so that I could succeed more quickly. Unfortunately, some of my teammates didn't see it that way and sort of voted him out of a coaching job at the end of the season," Bright said.

Nevertheless, Bright said, "He was the first instructor to see me on my first day on the ice with all the hockey gear on. He must've been laughing hysterically to himself! I was a very good skater, but I had never before carried a hockey stick or handled a puck. Today, he says I had a 'deer in the headlights' look in my eyes that day. He teases me in front of his students in the clinics (that I still take today) with that story, and tells them he had never seen a player advance as quickly as [I had] in three years." Bright believes her dedication and commitment to hockey come from within, but the knowledge to create the talent comes from that important first coach.

Rick Tekip, a student of Wisniewski's and the B squad's assistant coach, has a style completely opposite. He does not scream. According to Bright, "Tekip was the kinder, gentler, but firm coach. He was the one most of the players would go to if they didn't understand something, knowing that he would never belittle or embarrass them in front of others.

"He's very knowledgeable of the game and has helped me tremendously in the way of seeing the 'big picture.'" Bright said Tekip would be the first to have a "chalk talk with us and help us understand plays. He'd encourage us to watch tapes of our games and break them down."

Tekip may be more patient, but he admitted his own frustration about the attitude of some of the players. "With guys it's more like put up or shut up," he said, "but women want to know why. The magic word is *why*." Tekip said he loves to explain, and when he does that, "they don't want to hear it. They are inconsistent.

"I wish they had the same level of dedication as men," Tekip said. He complained that one player doesn't want to come to practices, but if a practice date gets changed to a game instead, she will come. He said some have the attitude that because they pay to play hockey, they don't have to practice. Tekip, who taught children and adult clinics before coming to the Ice, believes that girls who began playing team sports when very young understand the importance of dedication. Tekip joked about how bossy some of the women are. "They tell everybody what to do, including the coaches."

Bright's second season with the Ice brought new coaches: Tim Kaspar, 52, and his sidekick of more than 20 years, Joe Poremba, 40. She said, "Both men had coached teams from mites to junior but had never before coached women. It was definitely an experience for them. They obviously enjoy it, since they just completed their third season as our coaches."

For Kaspar, coaching women was an adjustment, according to Bright. "He's not a screamer, really, but he does yell. He's learned over the course of a season or two who he can yell at and who he can't. To some women, yelling pushes them to excel. To others, it hurts their game or makes them cry. He's become an expert on knowing which buttons to push and how hard to push them. Joe yells occasionally, but not often. He's stern when he's trying to get a point across. More often than not, yelling is reserved for the locker room after we played a horrible game!"

But, Bright insists, "all four of my coaches have helped me become a better player with their knowledge—which I continue to soak up like a sponge—and also with their encouragement. Sometimes I'd have phone conversations with former coach Larry before a game, just for inspiration. There were so many times that I wanted to quit the game, because I became frustrated with my rate of advancement. I wanted to be Wayne Gretzky in my first year. I wanted to run before I could crawl. I thought I was a terrible player. The coaches were inspirational in their efforts to boost my confidence—to a point where I literally saw it change my game. I never thought that mental attitude was a big part of success because hockey is primarily physical. But they kept drilling phrases like, 'When you step out on the ice, tell yourself that you are the best player out there.' Whether I was or not, they made me believe it. And they made the team believe it. We went from a losing team in 1997 to winning our division and tournament championships in 1999 and 2000."

Bright believes the coaches are the backbone of the team. "We lost, and they were with us in the bar after the game, reviewing plays with nickels, dimes, and pennies [representing the players] on the table. They will never know how much that helped me. Even if I couldn't be the dime. Tim and Joe are great communicators and created a team of 12 individuals that plays as one.

"Our coaches will be the last to admit that they have anything to do with our success. They think the players make the coach. I think the coaches make the players. It should be a big tip-off to them when they are getting dollar offers from men's teams who want them to coach their team. They are offered 'double what the women pay you.' " Bright said, "Tim told them they couldn't pay him enough. What the men's teams don't know is that our coaches are volunteers. We don't pay them a dime!"

Tekip's incentive to volunteer so much of his time is seeing the team improve. If players have an hour of practice, he puts in at least three hours, planning drills and game lines, getting to the rink early, talking to the team afterward. If they have a game, it's another three hours per game. When they travel, the whole weekend is dedicated to this. Although he sometimes has difficulties working with women, Tekip feels the rewards are greater than with men. He loves to teach, especially when his students are enthusiastic and eager listeners.

"Their dedication and commitment has produced a wonderful team," Bright said about the coaches. "We will continue to learn more, play harder, and, when Tim says, 'I will take you to the next level,' I can't wait!"

DO WOMEN HAVE TIME TO BE COACHES?

Greg Jayne, a sportswriter for the *Statesman Journal* in Salem, Oregon, wrote an article in 1999 about women coaching high school sports. A growing number of women are head coaches at the high school level in his area, he reported, yet they still are outnumbered by men by three to one.

Jayne wrote, "Those numbers are disconcerting to school administrators, who say that qualified female coaches are difficult to find and more difficult to keep. According to a female athletic director, 'women in athletics need to have coaching role models.'" Jayne pointed out that "in the role of developing athletes' physical and personal skills, coaches provide lessons that last a lifetime for both boys and girls. And while boys usually have male coaches who can serve as role models, girls less frequently find themselves under the tutelage of women they can emulate."

One student told the reporter, "a lot of female role models that people have are kind of too far away. They're really distant, like Mia Hamm. You don't get to know them on a personal basis; you don't get to talk to them. It's inspiring, but it's also unrealistic."

However, as the *Statesman Journal* article pointed out, a generation ago, schools often needed three or four head coaches to fill their staff. "Girls' sports were not prevalent, and boys' coaches would frequently lead two or three teams during a school year. Head coaches in Salem Keizer [school district] are paid anywhere from $2,770 to $6,129 in addition to their teaching salary, depending upon which sport they are in and their coaching experience. The scale is highest for football and boys' and girls' basketball, beginning at $3,694."

The pay is usually a flat fee, even if the team is successful and plays three or four postseason games in state play-offs. In most high schools around the country, good coaches put in many extra hours during the season. Then there are all kinds of extra events good coaches participate in, including coaching various all-star games and showcase games and making introductions to college coaches.

Of course, the logistics of coaching children plays a role here, too. Most team practices take place in the evening, and road trips often mean late-night returns home. Women teachers who have families may find this difficult unless they are married to men who share the responsibilities of the home. For example, one couple, both of whom are teachers and coaches, arrange their schedule so that one coaches fall and winter sports and the other handles spring sports.

In some instances, colleges are following the lead of corporate America by offering day care in an effort to lure female coaches. But at some high schools, which may require participation fees from the athletes simply to afford a team, such luxuries are not possible.

Reporter Jayne himself understands the time conflicts coaching can cause. He and his wife, volleyball coach Patty Jayne, planned their baby around Patty's coaching schedule.

ARE WOMEN GETTING THE JOBS?

According to Marc Bloom, himself a high school coach, writing in the *New York Times*, 87 percent of high school athletic directors are men, and these directors "tend to ignore qualified women for coaching positions in favor of men."

While the average number of women's collegiate teams per school is at a high, the percentage of women coaching them is the lowest ever. This is according to a study of intercollegiate athletics released in May 2000. This study has been conducted every two years by R. Vivian Acosta and Linda Jean Carpenter, retired physical education professors at Brooklyn College. When Title IX was enacted, more than 90 percent of women's team coaches were women. Now it's 45.6 percent, down a notch from 47.4 percent in 1998. This is reflected in professional sports, too. The WNBA began with a majority of women coaches, and within three years that majority was male. Today, only in volleyball are there more women coaches than there are men coaches. According to the American Volleyball Coaches Association in 1999, 58 percent of high school and college coaches are female, and 42 percent are male.

Of the 534 new jobs that came available for women's NCAA teams in 1998, women got only 107 of those coaching jobs. The number of female athletic directors has also declined, and in 23 percent of all women's athletic programs, there are no women anywhere in the athletic structure. At the same time, the number of women's and girls' teams is way up. From 1999 to 2000, 205 new women's teams were added to the NCAA. This is an average of 8.14 teams per school, up from about 2 per school in 1972.

Even in sports where there is a 50-50 ratio of male and female coaches, male coaches are more likely to have the highest paying jobs and the status positions at major institutions and therefore the budgetary, facility, recruiting, and staffing resources to maintain their successful and advantaged positions, according to the Women's Sports Foundation.

However, women are quickly rising in the ranks of assistant coaches. Two female head coaches in particular have worked their way up the ranks quickly. Stefanie Pemper spent her first coaching year at the University of Alaska as the assistant. She then spent two years as assistant at Idaho State and was assistant coach at Harvard for three years before coming to Bowdoin. She has coached all divisions. And Patty Jayne was assistant coach at the University of Oregon until she became head coach at the University of Portland.

ARE WOMEN COACHING BOYS AND MEN?

Joy McCarthy, an Atlanta, Georgia, corporate psychologist, said, "If I had another life, I'd love to come back as a coach." She did some coaching when her sons were young in the 1970s, but after they were out of the fifth grade she stopped because of her son's discomfort with his teammates making negative comments about the coach, his mother. McCarthy said if she was too aggressive the boys called her names behind her back, and this embarrassed her sons. "I did not find this to be a problem when coaching my daughter's team," McCarthy said. She used a strategy of letting every kid play (the goal of children's sports) but putting the weaker players in positions where they did less harm. When they won the city championship, the other coach said, "You outcoached me."

During the one year Linda Van Valkenberg coached boys' volleyball in addition to her usual stint as coach for girls' teams, she said, "I saw clear-cut differences in coaching boys and girls. It's easier to coach boys. First you have to gain their respect by showing them that you know how to play the game and also to coach it. You have to insist on their attention and let them know who's the boss right away or they will ignore you (especially if you are a woman). After that, it's easy."

"Men tend to think of players as machines. They try to get the machine right," said Carole Oglesby. She believes men and women have equal capacity to be good coaches. "Women have not been tried yet," she said and pointed to the fact that with rare exceptions, "women never get the chance to coach boys and men." She believes that if this were the case, male and female behavior would not be so dramatically different.

One of Oregon's athletic directors told reporter Greg Jayne the same thing, that we'll know "we have arrived when the women start coaching guys."

HELPING TO TRANSFORM COACHING FOR EVERYONE

The addition of women's teams into the sports arena is a signal that coaching is probably changing across the board. While women athletes are forcing coaches to treat them with respect, men's coaches may be changing, too.

Jere Longman wrote, "DiCicco's belief that women should be coached differently did not suggest a weakness in women as much as it underscored the increasing failure of methods used to coach men at the end of the century. The double-knit explosions of baseball managers who kicked dirt in sandbox apoplexy, the petulant stomping of basketball coaches, the cantilevered bellies of football coaches, unable to control their personal excesses, much less the excesses of their players."

Carole Oglesby believes "the best coaches are human beings who relate to human beings in a positive way."

Traditional male coaching styles may no longer be appropriate for men's teams and may cause male players to rebel as well. A man who played basketball as a college student at the University of Pennsylvania years ago cited the coach's behavior as the reason he quit the team. He could no longer tolerate the coach's "infantile" temper tantrums. "When he kicked a bucket of soda cans across the locker room after a poor performance by the team, I left." However, he never left his love of the game and today encourages his daughters. "They are great athletes," he said. "It's genetic!"

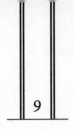
TITLE IX REVISITED:
MILES TO GO BEFORE WE SLEEP

~

"The day after the game, a lot of us who aren't so young anymore were trying to search the whole cluttered attic of our memories to try to think if there was ever a time when there had been a more exciting climax to an athletic event that had meant as much to so many. I'm not sure that in my lifetime there has been."

—PRESIDENT CLINTON TO THE U.S. WOMEN'S SOCCER TEAM AFTER THEIR WORLD CUP VICTORY. JERE LONGMAN, *NEW YORK TIMES*, JULY 20, 1999.

ANYONE WHO WANTS to know how close we are to achieving equality in sports can ask Nikki Dixon Leader of Denham Springs, Louisiana. In 1996, nearly 25 years after Title IX became law, Leader lost her job coaching girls' softball and girls' basketball at Denham Springs High School because she tried to get equal facilities for her girls' teams and equal pay for coaching those teams. Leader coached for nearly 20 years and brought a string of championships to the high school.

She is not alone in the continuing struggle for equality on the playing fields. In the year 2000, 28 years after Title IX changed the law, most high schools, and almost 80 percent of all educational institutions, are still not in compliance with the federal law with regard to athletic programs, according to the Women's Sports Foundation. During this period, the Office of Civil Rights (OCR) of the U.S. Department of Education has not initiated proceedings in even one case to withdraw federal funds from schools not in compliance. Male college athletes are still receiving $159 million more than women in athletic scholarships. Less than 9 percent of all Division I universities are considered to be in compliance with federal regulations of Title IX. The Women's Sports Foundation itself helps 750 students, parents, and coaches solve gender equity problems every year.

Nikki Leader admitted that when she first began teaching and trying to organize a girls' basketball team at a junior high school in 1971, she wasn't even aware that Title IX was about to change federal law and give girls equal access to sports—including money and facilities. This was the same year that a Connecticut judge who ruled against the rights of women to participate in sports said, "Athletic competition builds character in our boys. We do not need that kind of character in our girls, the women of tomorrow." Fortunately, he was overruled the following year by the passage of Title IX.

In 1972 Leader had gotten her girls' basketball team. "I did it [coaching] without pay," she said, "because I just loved the game so much." She had grown up playing softball and basketball with her sisters, encouraged by a father who never told them girls couldn't play ball. "I liked the game so much I didn't look into the profit motive. In looking back now," she said, "I see all the inequities."

How would she have known? When Title IX became law in the summer of 1972, it was almost totally ignored by the media and the sports establishment. It took three years to begin to gain attention as schools were being forced to spend money on women's sports.

In 1975 Leader moved from the junior high school to Denham Springs High School, where she was allowed to coach all girls' sports "as long as I didn't stir up any dust." Football was the focus of the school's athletic program—and money.

"With girls' sports we had to raise the money ourselves," she said. "My girls learned to be good salespeople." This was the same year that two powerful men's college football coaches, Bear Bryant of Alabama and Barry Switzer of Oklahoma, paid a visit to President Gerald Ford at the White House. They told the president they would not stand for this Title IX nonsense because it would take money away from football. The battle lines were drawn, and the lawsuits began.

In 1976 Yale women rowers stripped to the waist to create one of the most unusual protests against the lack of facilities for the women's team. Filmmaker Mary Mazzio's documentary *A Hero for Daisy*, released in 1999, is about the Yale women rowers' protest that sparked Title IX compliance action. Mazzio is a former Olympic rower and now a Boston lawyer. The film tells the story of Chris Ernst, a two-time Olympian who led her rowing team in a protest against Yale's lack of athletic facilities for women. Ernst and 18 teammates silently marched into Yale's athletic office, read a statement, and stripped to the waist exposing the words *Title IX*, which had been drawn in blue marker on each woman's back and breasts. A *New York Times* reporter stood behind the women observing the event. The next day the story appeared in the paper and set off an international reaction. Administrators recognized they had a problem concerning the legislation that had been enacted four years earlier.

But in a town in Louisiana, as Nikki Leader became more aware of the inequities, her own predicament was complicated by the politics of a small Southern town where everyone knows or is related to everyone else. Indeed, Leader's brother-in-law was the superintendent of schools, and his son, Leader's nephew, was the boys' basketball coach. Leader was also related to the principal of the high school. "The entire family is on the school board," Leader remarked. During this time, Leader was also going through a divorce from her husband.

However, Leader was building a strong girls' athletic program. Her teams had won two state high school softball championships. Twice she was regional coach of the year, twice she was nominated for national coach of the year.

"Both of my daughters played ball under me in high school," Leader said. My oldest daughter and I went to the Final Four twice while she was in high school in basketball, once in softball. My youngest daughter's basketball team won the state championship 39–0 when she was a junior. As a senior she went to the Final Four."

In 1989 school officials began to talk about building a new gym for the boys. Leader's concern that the girls would have unequal facilities was dismissed by the superintendent of schools (her brother-in-law), who said, "Oh, sure, we'll have a girls' gym." At the time, there was a field house and a gym at the school. Leader's girls' teams never had their own gym. While they had access to the weight room, it was located in the boys' gym, and the boys had priority. The men's coaches said of Leader, "She just wants the gym named for her."

Now Leader was getting really ticked off. She began expressing her concern about the inequality of facilities and her coaching pay. "I began going to meetings, speaking up," Leader said. "They told me that there was no money for a girls' gym, that they could only spend 1 million dollars." The final cost, she said, was 1.3 million dollars.

The first year the new gym opened, it was earmarked for boys' athetics and physical education classes only. According to Leader there were no dressing rooms or other facilities for girls.

Coaching salaries for girls' and boys' teams were equal on paper, Leader said, but the differences were made by Christmas bonuses. The athletic director got a $2,000 bonus; the boys' basketball coach got $1,000. Leader said she never got bonuses, which, she added, are illegal anyway. In addition, the boys could keep the money earned from the cola machines in the gym, while the girls had to sell candy and other things to raise money for their away games and trips.

Leader spent the next three or four years working her grievance through the system, taking the proper steps by writing letters to address her complaint to the school administration, the school board, and the federal Office of Civil Rights. When the regional OCR representatives came in from Dallas to visit Denham Springs High School, they claimed the only inequities they could find were that the boys had better gym bags—leather as opposed to cloth for the girls.

After the OCR debacle, Leader took her case to Katherine Wheeler, a Baton Rouge attorney, to sue the school district and plead her case with the federal Equal Employment Opportunity Commission (EEOC).

"We filed with the EEOC," Wheeler said, "but it takes two to three years to get the right to sue." Wheeler, who has handled other Title IX cases, said, "It's the nature of the area. It's a rural, ultra-conservative reactionary parish. It's a bedroom community." Wheeler said the regional OCR representatives at that time were "a bunch of functionaries."

Meanwhile, school officials took their revenge on Leader. After she had brought them two state championships, they took away her softball team in 1993 and had her coach track, which she didn't want to do. They warned Leader they would also take basketball away. Leader's daughter Leslie quit the softball team in sympathy for her mother.

From then on, there were years of harassment. School administrators called Leader on the carpet for every petty infraction—a cookie sheet had not been returned to the proper party in time after a social event at the school; she was 10 minutes late getting her team announcement into the office. They criticized her in front of the students and denegrated her in front of other teachers. In the teachers' lounge, with others around, the school principal (her ex-husband's nephew) complained about Leader's character, saying she was "real mean to players."

"She could not walk through the hallway," Wheeler said, "without being harassed." Using the cookie sheet as their excuse, the school administration took away her basketball coaching position in 1996. This was the team she had nurtured, her daughter was on it, and they were headed for the state championship. The following year they took away her office, then her physical education class. The administration gave three official reasons: 1) she did not return the cookie sheet in time, 2) she signed the name of the assistant coach to a purchase order, which Leader says was standard practice among all coaches, 3) she acted unprofessionally by getting a technical foul during a game.

"They put me into the classroom to teach health," Leader said. She had an offer from another school in a different parish, but she didn't want to go because she would miss her daughters' games, and she had worked with them since they were five years old. However, it was not easy to get another job close to home because some schools accused her of "carrying too much baggage." Leader eventually did move to a junior high school in another parish west of Baton Rouge. What she had to leave behind in Denham Springs were her tenure, her benefits, and her pride, as well as her winning teams. Since Leader left, the girls basketball team at Denham Springs High School has never gone to the play-offs.

"It was a travesty," Wheeler said. "It still is." The case was thrown out of the state appeals court and is now in federal appeals court. And there are scores of lawsuits like Leader's in the courts. The University of Iowa keeps tabs on Title IX lawsuits on its gender equity website.

~

Many women have experienced the same kind of arrogant and flagrant disregard for the law. Even 16 years after the law was changed, Zan Taylor, then coach of women's basketball at Columbia University, said, "Nobody enforced it. We went to Pepperdine in 1988. We were the away team and had been assigned to the gym for practice at a certain time. The men's coach [male] came in and said we couldn't play because, 'We [the men's team] have to practice.' They had no problem doing that. I felt betrayed as a coach. He had no respect for me as a coach," Taylor said, and her players "were so dejected."

Kathleen Connolly, 30, of Queens, New York, who went to St. John's University on a basketball scholarship in 1988 and until then had not experienced discrimination in women's sports, was rudely awakened.

"'Throw all the women out,' men's coach Lou Carnesecca would say. He wanted the gym empty." St. John's men got more playing time and better coaches during Connolly's time there. She was disappointed in college basketball after her exciting years at Christ the King High School, a Catholic school in Queens where it was a good thing to be a girl and a basketball player, and where Connolly was recruited by more than 300 colleges, including Stanford and the University of Connecticut.

"I didn't play much in college," she said, and it was a big letdown after being a superstar at Christ the King. She said the St. John's women's team won the eastern regional the year before she arrived, but the coaching staff changed in the interim.

When Mary McNichol attended the University of Pennsylvania, she was stunned by "a huge gap" between the men's and women's athletics. "There was no training room or training tables. The money we got for lunch or dinner at away games was paltry. I vaguely remember getting about four dollars for dinner for an away game and that the men got ten dollars or so, and, of course, they ate at the training table every night, which was off-limits to women athletes. The basketball coach was a woman who had never been a player." McNichol, who had grown up playing sports with her four sisters and had been encouraged by her dad, had no idea until then that it wasn't always cool to be a woman and play sports.

McNichol and current soccer teammate Gail Lipstein were both athletes at the University of Pennsylvania from 1969 to 1973 as Title IX was coming into law. As president of the Women's Athletic Association, Lipstein went to meetings with the department. She asked for sneakers and a locker room.

"Well, you have uniforms," they told her, as if to ask what more she could want. "The uniforms were from the '50s," Lipstein said, "the old tunic style. The field hockey team had to buy their own shirts. Every sport required us to buy our own shoes. Without locker rooms, we had a hallway with open cages in the middle of a stairwell. Everybody was coming and going. When we asked to use the men's training room, they were aghast. 'You can't go into the men's training room.'

"The athletic director didn't give a darn about women's sports. There was no money," Lipstein said.

Sue Nesbihal played at college in the first year of Title IX and recalls the abrupt change in some conditions. "We had to sell fortune cookies," she said, to raise money for team shirts. "And the next year we had uniforms for home and away games. We went from the coach buying us a hamburger, to $7.50 for meals." She said, "We didn't know how to spend it." Nesbihal recalled traveling to an away game and staying in a real hotel for the first time. The basketball team used to ride to games in two station wagons, but by 1972 they had a bus. Nesbihal had offers of scholarships, but she said in those days, "you had to play several sports." There was no scholarship for girls for one sport. A few years after she graduated, she was offered a job as women's athletic director at Old Westbury, a Long Island campus of the State University of New York.

"My job would be to turn on the lights for the boys' program, sweep up the floor when we were done for the men to play. All for half the pay of the men's athletic director."

"You can follow Title IX and still give no support," said volleyball coach Patty Jayne, pointing out that there was no money for marketing or training at the University of Portland, where she was head coach in the late 1990s. It affected the players. "The athletic director said, 'Don't even think about it,' when I asked for more support. We tried to get respect by doing well. We finished fifth or sixth. I'm a competitor; what am I supposed to do here? I just couldn't compromise. The University of Portland was a Division I school, but for 10 years they had only an average team," said Jayne. "They didn't care about the women's program. I was naive and arrogant enough to think I could change it," she said. Jayne, who went to a Catholic girls' high school, was not used to playing second fiddle to the boys.

Jayne's sister, Anna Maria Lopez, went to that same Catholic girls' school, and she remembers a very positive effect. In 1973, sports at St. Mary's Academy in Portland, Oregon, took off with a boom, right after Title IX, and the following year Lopez was a high school freshman there.

Lopez was an All-American in basketball and softball in high school. She also competed in track and was a two-time champion discus thrower who went to the University of Southern California as a two-sport athlete. She was recruited in high school and said she "felt sort of cocky." In college, Lopez was All-American in volleyball and played for USA Volleyball. She currently plays with an adult division of USA Volleyball and participates in regional competitions. At 40, she is the second oldest player on the team.

St. Mary's Academy, the oldest secondary school in Oregon, was founded by 12 courageous French Canadian nuns who sailed around Cape Horn from Montreal, Canada. The oldest of these nuns was 30, and they opened their school with six students, but not all were Catholic. Their mission was education for all. There are now 525 students, down from 720 when Anna Maria was a student; 98 percent go to college, and 60 percent are athletes. The sports teams, known as "The Blues," have won 14 state championships. Volleyball is their strongest sport.

"Then we played because it was fun," said Lopez, who is now athletic director of that school, recalling the days before Title IX. "Title IX upped the ante. Now, athletes are under pressure to get scholarships." She points out the pressure is often from parents who see the financial advantage, and it's also about status. "It's a whole identity thing," she said. There is more visibility now and more recognition and opportunity. The girls at St. Mary's play all year and in several sports.

GOING UNDERGROUND

In the past 20 years, the Women's Sports Foundation claims, it appears that antidiscrimination laws have driven discriminatory treatment, policies, and practices underground as opposed to eliminating such conduct. They are more difficult to uncover, more artful, more deceiving, like the fuss made over that cookie sheet in Denham Springs, Louisiana.

Of the 100 schools in Division I-A, the premier competitive league of the National Collegiate Athletic Association (NCAA), there are only four women heading programs that serve both male and female athletes. Eight women head programs governing only women's athletics.

These four women sit between the proverbial rock and a hard place, according to the Women's Sports Foundation. If they make an effort to improve the record of their schools in the area of gender equity, they will be accused of favoring women because they are women. If anything goes wrong with men's sports, they face an "I told you so; women can't do this" attitude. Or, tough decisions are taken out of their hands, as in the case of Michigan State, where, when the football coach needs to be replaced, this important responsibility is taken away from the female athletic director and assumed by the male president. The Women's Sports Foundation poses the question: Would this be the case if the athletic director were male?

SHOW US THE MONEY

Women's college basketball coaches' (both male and female) average base salary was found to be $42,000 compared to $77,000 for head coaches of men's basketball (who are all men), according to a survey of head coaches of NCAA Division I basketball teams. More than 73 percent of head coaches of men's basketball make a base salary of more than $60,000, while just 27 percent of head coaches of women's basketball make more than $60,000. This is according to a 1998 survey by the Women's Basketball Coaches Association, which also reports that while 90 percent of head coaches of men's

NCAA Division I basketball have employment contracts, a mere 75 percent of head coaches of women's NCAA Division I basketball have contracts.

According to the March 1997 *Chronicle of Higher Education,* a study conducted by the University of Texas reveals that NCAA Division I-A men's basketball coaches were the highest paid individuals in college sports in 1996–97 with median compensation of $290,000. Women's NCAA Division I-A basketball coaches had median compensation of $98,400. The median salary for a softball coach ($44,725) is 56 percent of that for a baseball coach ($79,570).

In 1997 the NCAA predicted that it would take another 10 or 12 years to achieve equality in women's and men's programs. In 1998 they cut that prediction in half because more women are participating. The number of women in Division I athletics increased by 28 in each school compared to an increase of 15 for men. Women account for about 40 percent of Division I athletes compared to 37 percent two years ago. Women attending Division I schools received 41 percent of the scholarship dollars.

The average recruiting budget for women in Division I schools is $72,000 compared to $172,000 for men, according to the Carpenter and Acosta annual report that tracks compliance to federal law.

WHAT CAN WE DO?

The public can contribute to the move toward gender equity by encouraging states to change their laws. At least 20 states have either passed legislation or have legislation pending for the purpose of improving gender equity in college athletics. At least five states have provided monetary assistance to schools within the state university system in the form of tuition waivers to increase the number of opportunities for female student athletes. Some states have provided funding to schools to build better facilities for women's athletics.

Some important changes have come about because people have been vocal about unfair practices they have seen. For example, while some schools and recreation centers continue to bully women off the court, the University of Iowa has established some rules to ensure gender equity by designating some courts "priority for women." Men can also use the courts, but they must yield should women wish to play. The rules were developed as a result of a complaint that was filed with the University of Iowa Recreation Services. The University of Iowa website also maintains a comprehensive national gender equity report.

Even with changes like those at the University of Iowa, there is still a great deal of work to be done. According to the Women's Sports Foundation, in recent years, eight major studies have been completed concerning gender equity in college athletics. Each of these studies came to basically the same conclusion: although improvements have been made in recent years, colleges and universities are still a long way from complying with the regulations of Title IX.

The Women's Sports Foundation estimates that at the current rate it will take at least another 10 years for the majority of schools to comply with a federal law that was passed almost 30 years ago. To help move the process along, they urge us all to put pressure on our Congressional representatives, write letters to the media, and join grassroots organizations in support of promoting women's sports.

PART III

Transforming Our Lives

10

FROM SEX OBJECTS
TO ACTION FIGURES

~

"I don't like this 'fear of being big' thing because it falls into the general
female thing of wanting to be less—less powerful, less assertive,
less demanding, less opinionated, less present, less big."

—From *Big Girl in the Middle*, by Gabrielle Reece and Karen Karbo

Kelly Kennedy was six feet tall by the time she was 13 and was often the target of cruel teasing by her less vertically gifted classmates. In addition to being taller than her peers and her older brother, she was overweight and uncoordinated—a klutz with no natural athletic ability. Today, at 22, Kelly is six feet four and a volleyball champion. She stands tall and walks proudly, her self-esteem obvious to the people who are attracted to her because they know she is somebody special.

It didn't come easy, but Kennedy's story is one with which any girl who doesn't fit the female social stereotype can identify. It's a story of being "different" at a time when that is the worst possible thing you can be. And it is a story of the power of being part of a sports team. In a less loving family or another time or place, Kennedy might never have had the opportunity to gain a sense of self or learn to be proud of her body. She was fortunate to have a supportive family, but she was also a fighter who persisted against heavy odds.

Because her parents, Bill and Patricia Kennedy, loved sports, they encouraged their daughter to try out for middle school teams. In the seventh and eighth grades in Barrington, Illinois, an affluent suburb outside Chicago, Kennedy tried out for the volleyball team, but she failed miserably. She did not make any team. In high school, she was accepted onto the B volleyball team. However, the team was coached by the cheerleading coach, who had never played volleyball herself. Kennedy was unable to learn much about the game or about how she could improve her ability. She was demoralized, her dad said, and her self-esteem suffered.

Pat and Bill Kennedy knew their daughter needed more than just her parents' encouragement, so they took her to the Sports Performance Club in West Chicago, a top training ground for athletes. There she tried out for the volleyball team with 76 other hopefuls. While Bill watched his daughter "crashing and burning" before his eyes, he thought there was no way she would be picked for this elite program.

"She was slouching; she wasn't fast," Bill Kennedy said. However, coach Rick Butler proved them wrong. Taking Kennedy's hand, Butler raised her arm to see how far she could reach. He told Kennedy she had something he needed that he could not buy or train. She had height. Butler also told her that if she were willing to make the commitment and work hard, he would make a volleyball player out of her.

When Kennedy's parents asked her if she was willing to give up everything to make that kind of commitment, she said, "I have nothing to give up." Her academic life was miserable and her social life worse. At Barrington High School, the kids never invited Kennedy to their parties. She did not fit in.

Kennedy made the commitment. She trained four and a half hours a day, six days a week. She lifted weights, ran, did the workouts, did the drills. She got up at 6 A.M. every day and went to school. After school Pat would pick her up and drive the hour to the club where she would train from four until 9 P.M. before going home to do her homework until midnight.

"I drove her every day," Pat said. "We ate in the car. I used to sit in the parking lot five or six hours in the snow. It was easier than making that long trip twice. The car became home. I brought my bills, read the newspaper, made phone calls." But more important to Pat was the precious time those long drives gave mother and daughter. "I got a lot closer to Kelly. In the car together she would talk, open up, especially about how she felt about the teasing. She told me about a boy in school who called her 'Ogre.' He taunted her because she wasn't having fun and going to parties like the other kids. When Kelly told him she was going to get a scholarship, he laughed at her. I'd like to know what he's doing now," Pat said.

"Kelly was the worst athlete Sports Performance ever had," Pat said, "but because she was not a natural athlete, she worked harder. Kelly never gave up. I remember seeing her almost in tears one day, on the sidelines of the gym with the coach teaching her footwork over and over again. All the other players were much better, but they soon learned that whatever Kelly may have lacked in natural ability, she overcame with persistence until she got it right." When the team wanted to find a way to compliment her, they said she hadn't stepped on anyone all week.

At Sports Performance they gave Kennedy immediate and long-term goals. The immediate goal was to lose weight; the long-term goals were the scholarship and the Olympics. "She never had goals before," Pat said, bragging that Kennedy got offers from 100 colleges, went to the University of Wisconsin on a full scholarship, made All-American twice, and hopes to make the Olympics in 2002. In four years, Kennedy turned her life around. It improved in all areas. Her grades went from Cs and Ds to As and Bs.

Today, Kennedy is a middle blocker on the Dream Team of United States Professional Volleyball (USPV), an organization spearheaded by her father. "I saw what a change [volleyball] made in my daughter's life," Bill Kennedy said. "And she's not the only one out there. It's the 17,500 college girls; it's the 260,000 club players and the two million in high school."

"That's the purpose of a parent," said this man who is no longer taller than his daughter, "to be sure your kids are happy and strong in their sense of self." Bill Kennedy said that his niece, who would never admit to being six feet tall—only five feet eleven—is no longer ashamed to own up to her true height because she sees how proud Kelly Kennedy feels.

A few years ago, Kennedy began dating a young man who came to one of her games; they have been dating ever since. He is as tall as Kelly, and when she wears high heels ("I'm already tall, what's a little more?") "he seems to elongate," her mother said, laughing. He plays on a club team and coaches kids' volleyball. With training and travel and exhibition games, Kennedy's life is taken up with volleyball. But when she can relax, she enjoys the company of her Siamese cat, Koshka, and listening to country music—or enjoying other sports like horseback riding, rafting, and skiing.

Kelly Kennedy is a strong woman, and she knows how fortunate she is because, she said, "I can't think of anybody who isn't supportive." But she did the work, and she achieved what she once would have thought impossible. Now when she walks into any room and the usual questions are asked—How tall are you? Do you play basketball?—she can smile and feel good when she answers. The people who ask look at her in awe.

"Five people came over to our table in a restaurant yesterday to talk," Pat Kennedy said, unable to hide her pride in her daughter. That Kelly Kennedy has achieved self-esteem is obvious.

"Volleyball is a beautiful, graceful sport," said Pat. "It was made for women. I was just thinking that as I watched practice yesterday." These women are not making as much money as they would playing in Europe, but they're doing it for future players.

~

Playing volleyball during their teens also gave the three Oden sisters a positive feeling about being tall—and led them all to Olympic history. All played on various medal-winning teams in the 1988, 1992, and 1996 Olympics. And all three and one brother are more than six feet tall.

At a Fourth of July Marine Corps picnic in Irvine, California, fate led Kim Oden, then 13, to the sport that would lead her and her two sisters to the Olympics. On this particular day, her father, a sports lover and Marine, ran into a buddy whose daughter was playing volleyball with a local club and invited Oden to join her. Kim was already close to her adult height of six feet three and had a strong, athletic body.

"It could have been anything," Oden recalled about the sport that put her on her life's path. It so happened that Oden enjoyed playing volleyball, and her father not only encouraged her, but made sure she got to all the practices. Her mom, while not an athlete herself, encouraged Kim, too. Eventually, Kim's two younger sisters,

Elaina and Bev, followed in her footsteps. Elaina remembered watching the 1976 Olympics on TV and saying, "Boy, I'd like to do that." By then it was not just a fantasy. "I had lots of insight into how to do it," Elaina said, because she had watched her sister.

"Elaina is the true athlete," Kim said about her sister, who is four years younger. "She lettered in all sports in school—basketball, track, soccer, volleyball." All three sisters were recruited for college. Kim went to Stanford University on a scholarship and with that volleyball team went to the Final Four four times. Bev later won a scholarship to Stanford and Elaina went to Pacific University.

Kim played in the 1988 Olympics in Korea and in 1992 was joined in Spain by her sister Elaina. They came home with bronze medals. In 1996 Elaina and Bev played in the Olympics.

"I don't know if they knew how far we would go," Kim said about her parents. Her dad came to the first Olympics in Korea. The whole family traveled to Spain in 1992 and shared the Olympic moment with Kim and Elaina. The entire extended family came to the Atlanta games in 1996 to see Elaina and Bev.

Elaina is now assistant volleyball coach at the Indiana University, a Big Ten school, but a knee injury finished her playing career. She needs a new knee, she said, but "I'll hold out until the technology is better." She admits the injury occurred when she was training with the national team and had not warmed up enough and landed wrong on her knee.

Of the three Oden sisters, only Bev did not pursue a career in coaching sports. Kim began her coaching career once she stopped playing, starting as an assistant volleyball coach at the University of North Carolina. From North Carolina she moved on to Duke University and later Iowa State. She is now the assistant coach at Stanford, her alma mater.

DREAMING DREAMS AND SETTING GOALS

"I just wanted to walk in," Diane Ratnik said with great passion about the dream she had when she was 14 to play in the Olympics, "and to travel the world." She made that dream a goal—and then a reality. Ratnik began playing volleyball in the eighth grade with the goal to get to the Olympics by the time she was 18. In 1981 she received a scholarship to the University of Michigan and later was asked to join Team Canada. She played full-time—six hours a day, six days a week—and competed in the 1984 Olympics. She retired in 1988. Then she played pro volleyball for a short-lived Minneapolis league with six teams that began in 1987 and played three seasons of three months each. Once the league ended, after buying a car and with nothing left to live on, Ratnik moved back to Toronto and got a job in sports marketing, managing events.

"I still had a bug to play in the Olympics," Ratnik said, figuring she would be 34 in 1996. "I had a burning desire to go back, but I was an old dog learning new tricks." In 1996 in Atlanta she was the second-oldest player, but she discovered, "My body went into autopilot." Ratnik accomplished her goal—twice—and now gives motivational talks about goal setting through sports. She does clinics in schools and teaches kids the basics of volleyball.

Kathleen Connolly reached all but two of her goals by the time she was 30. Connolly, who said she grew up with a ball in her hand, was fortunate to go to Christ the King High School, in Queens, New York, noted for its girls' basketball program and its most famous graduate, Chamique Holdsclaw. Connolly was recruited by 300 colleges and chose St. John's University in New York.

Connolly's love of basketball came from her dad, now 65, who was recruited by colleges before the army sent him to Korea. However, he coached the community Catholic Youth Organization teams and passed his enthusiasm to his daughter and two sons. Connolly said she was never told she couldn't play sports because she was a girl, just because she was too little.

"She had some arm," her mother, Joyce Adamson, said, describing Connolly's early ability to throw a ball across the street. "When she was four she broke a window in the school." Connolly was called "Sonny" as a kid. Her hair was cut short because she was always sweaty. Her friends were all from the teams she played, "so I never felt any different," she said.

Connolly and her friends were impatient to play organized sports even though no teams were available until the eighth grade. When she asked her mom what sports she could play, Adamson told Connolly she could play anything she wanted except football. So, although they were not yet in eighth grade, "Kathleen and her friend went to the priest at school and asked for teams," Adamson recalled. "I told them I was only joking." Nevertheless, Adamson urged the school to start a girls' team. By the fifth grade, Connolly was allowed to play with the older teams. She played center field on the softball team although the older girls considered her a nuisance.

Connolly's brother TJ taught her how to read stats with a Strat-O-Matic game in the house. And they followed all the local games. New York Yankees shortstop Bucky Dent was her hero during high school, and she actually cried when Thurman Munson retired. TJ was the first in the family to go to Christ the King, and Connolly was always there at his games. She knew she wanted to go there, too.

Now a physical education teacher working toward her master's degree, she looks back on her high school and college career and acknowledges some regret about not going to the University of Connecticut, where she thinks she might have enjoyed more competition and better coaching. "Auriemma really wanted me," Connolly recalled with a wistful grin, referring to the University of Connecticut women's team coach. She realizes now that she probably should have gone to Connecticut to play on a team that was admired rather than scorned and has since won two national championships and produced several WNBA athletes such as Rebecca Lobo and Kara Wolters. But she wanted to stay near home, so she chose St. John's. At the time, Connolly also wanted to be closer to her boyfriend, Jeff, whom she eventually married.

Connolly still plays in several basketball leagues, including one on Long Island with former college players and WNBA New York Liberty trainer Lisa White. She also plays softball in bar leagues. She's a shortstop like her old hero, Bucky Dent.

Connolly firmly believes sports has kept her life on track, and she has reached all her goals, except for owning a house and receiving her master's degree. She and her husband, Jeff, have a daughter, Krista, and a son, Jeffrey, who was born in June 2000. Krista is four and already plays soccer in games videotaped by Jeff. Connolly hopes Krista will go to Christ the King High School and carry on the legacy.

"Am I pushing her? It would bother me if she doesn't play," Connolly remarked, with a worried look. "What'll I do?"

BODY PRIDE AND ADOLESCENCE

Connolly, Kennedy, and the Oden sisters had supportive families and the will to persist. The important thing was they got involved in sports at a time when it was crucial to develop a positive image of themselves and their bodies. As all of us who have been there know, as a teenager, it is horrible to be different in any way, to not fit in. And while boys have always had their "club" of sports in which to belong, until recently girls did not. So all those surging hormones of adolescence, all that power and energy, was squelched or diverted into waiting for him to call, trying not to beat him at bowling or the math exam, and learning how to dress and flirt. This energy burns inward as obsession with the body's appearance (manifested in bulimia and anexoria) instead of the body's power, physical strength, and confidence.

During puberty girls get a suddenly diminished body image that leads to low self-esteem no matter how tall or short they are. If self-consciousness isn't about height, it's about weight, or the shape of a nose, or breasts that are too small or too large. Tall women are told (or get the silent message) they won't find a husband, so they slouch and stoop to hide their height. If a girl's breasts develop out of proportion to the rest of her, she covers them with baggy clothing or carries her books crushed to her chest. The old standard that still exists is that girls and women are judged by their looks. We must be perfect and beautiful or we are not women.

Little boys see their like images on television and in photos in the sports section and know from their parents and friends that they are expected to play sports. They receive balls, gloves, and sports equipment by the age of two. Research shows that boys and girls between the ages of six and nine—and their parents—are equally interested in sports participation. However, as girls reach puberty, they receive subtle and not-so-subtle messages from everyone around them, and by the age of 14, girls drop out of sports at a significantly greater rate than boys.

But fathers can help change this pattern. Having an encouraging dad around during the teen years does a lot to help girls get through these years of doubts about their body image. A study by researchers at Loyola University of Chicago reveals that girls who are encouraged in sports by their dads are less likely to have eating disorders. Joe Kelly founded Dads and Daughters after one of his daughters asked him if he thought she was fat. Kelly's organization is educating fathers about their role in their daughters' self-esteem. Dads and Daughters also pressures the media to remove advertisements that make girls worry about their looks.

Until recently, girls and women simply did not receive the same opportunities as boys to play or the same positive reinforcement about sports participation. And still, go into any toy store and the first question a clerk will ask you is whether you are shopping for a boy or a girl. If you are browsing in the sports department, you are likely to be asked how big "he" is or what sport "he" plays. Toy stores are divided up into pink and blue. Boys' sections carry sporting goods and lots of toy soldiers and toy guns. Girls' aisles show Barbie and tea sets and toy kitchens and cut-out dolls. While Barbie now has costumes to show that she can be a doctor—even a basketball player—these specialty dolls don't sell nearly as well as the stereotypical Barbie in her shorts and tight shirt.

Some toys, of course, have crossed the gender barrier, but these are mostly computer-geared inventions such as Pokémon and Digimon. *Unisex* may be a big word at the Gap or at your hair-cutting salon, but it just isn't so in the toy stores. Only a few sporting goods stores carry the licensed products of the WNBA or the Women's National Soccer Team—or any teams that are less well known. The good news is that teenaged girls—and many boys—now admire Mia Hamm as much as they admire Michael Jordan. In fact, Nintendo produced the first video game about women's sports, a game that features Mia Hamm, action figure.

NO LONGER BEING OBJECTIFIED

Even when boys attend girls' games, they often stoop to criticizing physical attributes in their taunts and slurs. "Look at those boats," or "Are those skis?" about long feet, they yell from the stands. If a girl has broad shoulders, they might yell for her to go on a diet. Short hair, like a buzz cut, will draw catcalls like, "You got a guy on the team there."

Tamika Catchings, University of Tennessee six feet one junior, has a hearing impairment that meant she had to wear large hearing aids until she was in junior high school. Because the kids teased her, she stopped wearing them. At Tennessee games she always had to ask teammates what coach Pat Summitt was shouting. Now, able to use smaller aids, Catchings is more comfortable with the condition. And she can definitely hear Summitt's yells.

"I still watch myself getting anxious about being feminine," said Joy McCarthy, a psychologist who played sports as a child and in college. She recalled getting ready for a game—the stretching and warm-up exercises. "I was always aware of standing and making sure I looked feminine. But those who play basketball today don't worry about it," she said.

Carole Oglesby recalled a day in her teen years when she was all decked out in Bermuda shorts and new socks and feeling really cool. "Some of the guys commented that I had football legs." Such a remark could have devastated many girls. Fortunately, Oglesby had a supportive family, and so she did not give up her interest in sports. However, like all women who grew up in those dark ages, she understands how girls and young women felt when something they were trying to do was mocked. After all, she remembers that remark to this day. Oglesby did not continue to play softball because there were no opportunities to play at her level of skill; therefore, what was available was not much fun. "I still miss it," she said. However, Oglesby coached softball for a few years after college and directed her physical energy into jogging and skiing.

This self-consciousness of how we look is a big women's issue, even for women who are involved in sports. I doubt many men think about "looking masculine" as they play, but as women, we are so used to being objectified that we do it to ourselves, "watching" ourselves to be sure we're making the "right impression." Involvement in sports can change this because a girl is focused on the game rather than her body.

"Once they are on the floor they see themselves as athletes. They're not worried about their hair or their clothes," said Anna Maria Lopez, athletic director of a Catholic girls' high school in Oregon. "There's something about being able to perform in front of other people." Lopez believes this is easier for girls in a single-sex school. "They have a lot more confidence."

The beauty of sports is that it increases self-esteem at an age when girls traditionally lose self-esteem. Physical competence creates a sense of self-mastery and strength. A girl can make a decision from a position of strength, something boys learn as small children and carry with them throughout their lives. Whether a boy is short or tall, black or white, if he excels in sports, he is accepted by all.

In the past, exercise for adolescent girls was restricted to gym class or jumping up and down as a cheerleader for the boys' teams who were getting a real physical workout. How many girls were turned on by gym class, with its regimen of calisthenics or aerobics, which had no apparent goal or focus? Not to mention those awful gym suits! In the spirit of adolescent rebellion, they looked for any excuse not to participate. Girls grew up to be sedentary women. However, beating the other team or winning a school championship or getting an athletic scholarship to a good college would interest a girl enough to make physical fitness a big part of her life today—and raise her self-esteem.

A member of the Amherst, Massachusetts, girls' high school basketball team that was portrayed so memorably in Madeleine Blais's book *In These Girls, Hope Is a Muscle* perhaps summed up all that it means to be a teenager and an athlete when she said, "Madonna is not my hero. She wanted attention, she wanted money, she wanted glory, she wanted the microphone, and she did it just by taking off her clothes. I treat my body 300 degrees different. I lift weights not so I'll look strong to other people, but so I'll *be* strong. I take care of my body. I make sure I sleep. I sleep a lot more than my friends. I eat well . . . too much sugar, but other than that I'm fine. If I get an injury like a pull, I listen to it. I don't drink; I don't smoke. I ask enough of my body without asking it to deal with random substances. Once she got hold of the microphone, she just took off more clothes. She never did anything except be sexy. I resent the message that if you are sexy, you are powerful. That's what I think Madonna stands for. As an athlete, it kills me."

GROWING UP TO BE CONFIDENT WOMEN

"I was too involved with basketball," said Kathleen Connolly about why she rarely dated. When a boy asked her out in the eighth grade she said, "I've got basketball." This was her reason also for never smoking or doing drugs. "I knew it wasn't good."

A survey released in 1998 by the Women's Sports Foundation found that girls who play sports in school have sex later and don't get pregnant in their teen years as often as girls who are not involved in sports.

According to the President's Council on Physical Fitness and Sports in 1997, female high school athletes tend to get better grades than the girls who are not involved in sports. They are also less likely to drop out of school than girls who are not athletic. They are more likely to go to college and will develop fewer chronic health problems such as heart disease or high cholesterol. The report also indicated that girls who participate in sports are more mentally fit and develop social skills more easily than less-active girls.

"Softball was the first life skill where I learned what it meant to be good at something," said sports psychologist Carole Oglesby, who played softball as a teenager in California.

When you grow up proud of your body and feeling physically strong it stays with you for life. Kim Many, a 28-year-old corporate attorney in New York who plays recreational basketball with the New York Urban Professionals Athletic League, said, "I have always played team sports, and I think that it helped to define who I am. I did not have to rely on other things such as how much attention I received from boys or peers in high school because I was always in the [news]paper for my athletic prowess. Without team sports, I would not be the same confident individual that I am today. Excelling in athletics gives me confidence in other areas in my life."

Elizabeth McCarthy, 32, who plays in the same basketball league, said, "When I began playing on my high school team, there was a radical transformation. I didn't feel like an outsider anymore, which I did prior to that. It gave me an identity with a group of fun people and kept me from only being a shy, smart girl. It was also a place where it was not only OK to be tall, it was great, so I think it made me much more comfortable with myself physically."

"The better I do in athletics, the better I feel about myself," said Indiana University volleyball player Laura Mettes, 21. "I definitely have more self-confidence. Being an athlete at a major Division I university defines who you are. People that I don't even know will come up and say 'nice game' or 'I saw you on TV.' At first it was weird, but you get used to it."

And even if you didn't begin in childhood or adolescence, sports can take you to a new plateau, obvious from the stories of many women in this book. Cynthia Powell, a 34-year-old public relations professional in Washington, D.C., said she never thought of herself as an athlete. "I was late walking, riding a two-wheeler, always the last one picked, so I got the message that I wasn't coordinated." Powell, who has been rowing on the Potomac River with Alexandria Community Rowing for more than two years, said, "I think a lot of it was about confidence." She laughed about having no hand-eye coordination. "There's no ball involved [in rowing]," she said. "I still struggle with my image as an athlete. I don't think of myself as an athlete. My body has changed. I have more upper-body strength. My legs are toned and stronger. I used to have back problems. I'm not sure it's the rowing that did it, but I feel better.

"I had never done it before," Powell said, about the idea of "trying as hard as I can." She said she had done this intellectually, and with academics, but not as an athlete. She rows with a group that includes a few younger women just out of college who are very strong. "I have a constant dialogue in my head—am I holding the others back? I really struggle with this."

One of Powell's challenges was taking the coxswain position. "We rotate coxing," she said, "and I always made excuses. The river is intimidating." But Powell, like a good sport, finally took her turn, and her confidence was put to the supreme test when her boat crashed into another. "I didn't know enough about coxing to know if it [the accident] was my fault." Powell said the coach is generally a great guy but had his annual temper blowup that day. He screamed at both coxswains. Powell may have been intimidated by the river, the crash, and the screaming coach, but the negatives carried less weight than what rowing with a team had taught her. "I had to put my feelings aside. I had to do my job and get my boat back to the dock. There was not time to worry about whether it was my fault." As another rower told her later, "It happens; don't take it personally."

Katie Kauffman, a member of the U.S. Women's National Field Hockey Team, said, "You learn how to sacrifice for the good of the team. I have become more confident in almost everything I have tried," she said. "I have become more of a leader and more creative as a team player. I have also come to appreciate what my body will enable me to do and have become much more complacent with my body and how it looks. I have struggled with eating disorders in the past but have learned how to take care of my body before it became a huge setback for me as a professional athlete."

Mary McNichol, who began playing soccer in her 40s, remembered how her earlier sports activity affected her life. "Sports saved my life," McNichol said, describing a period between college and career when she was adrift and feeling depressed. "I recalled that in college, when I played on a basketball team, I had to show up for practice and for games no matter how I felt, and that brought it back to me. I realized I needed that discipline in my life and that it worked for me. Playing sports kept me sane."

Ice hockey player Jen Stitzell said, "It's made me more confident in myself and confident with strangers. I feel like I stick up for myself more now than I did before I played hockey. I love getting out daily aggressions on the ice. It really relieves stress and is a great escape from everyday life."

Oglesby belives there are many women today, especially professional women, who know that it is important that their daughters get the opportunity to play team sports.

A FAMILY ASSET

"Sports are also a family asset," Oglesby said, "that creates a shared goal and a nurturing experience"—as witnessed by Kelly Kennedy, the Oden sisters, Kathleen Connolly, Rhonda Taylor, Mavis Albin, and so many women in this book.

"My family is another amazing group of supporters," Katie Kauffman, member of the U.S. Women's National Field Hockey Team, said. "My dad saved all his vacation days to take day trips to see me and my team play." Kauffman's family went to the 1999 Pan Am games in Winnipeg, Canada, and went to England for the qualifying tournament. In 1996 they were in Atlanta, Georgia, for the Olympics for two and a half weeks. "They have been to just about every state in the USA watching me play. And they mostly drive," Kauffman said.

"Most of our competition is overseas, so that is why we have to venture to foreign countries quite often. My passport has two pages left," Kauffman said. "My mom is afraid to fly, but when she has to cross bodies of water, she has no choice but to fly. So she will either take Tylenol PM to help her sleep or a stronger source of sleeping pills. She also sits on the aisle and tries to relax by talking to others. The fact that I fly all the time and haven't had any horror stories has kept her calm as well." Kauffman said her boyfriend also scrimps for money to travel to cheer on her and the team.

Kris Fillat, also a member of the U.S. Women's Field Hockey Team, said she has been on the team for 10 years and away from her family a great deal of time. "I am the only one from California on the team, so I was usually the only one with no one there to watch when we played. But ever since we train in San Diego, they have been able to see me play so much more and have really gotten into it. They all came to the Atlanta Olympics, and my mom, stepdad, and my brothers-in-law came to the Pan Ams in Winnipeg, Canada. I couldn't believe they spent the money to go there. My mom has even become one of those crazy pin collectors that you see at all the tournaments."

LEAVING NO GIRL OUT

Girls in poor families are less likely to have the opportunity to play sports, according to the Tucker Center for Research on Girls & Women in Sport at the University of Minnesota. Among the poor, women may not have time for sports, because they are holding down several jobs and caring for children. There are also intangibles—such as cultural attitudes and traditions about femininity, competition, and aggression—that keep women from participating.

The popularity of the Women's World Cup soccer team was the start of gender equalization, but the cities haven't kept pace with the suburbs in developing teams, partly because they lack the open spaces. World Cup corporate sponsors hope to turn city girls into soccer players, too, particularly immigrant girls who come from male-dominated countries. Urban Soccer Girl Programs, including skills clinics, have opened up in six cities—Boston, Massachusetts; Chicago, Illinois; Los Angeles, California; Portland, Oregon; San Francisco, California; and Washington, D.C. The goal of the clinics is to introduce soccer to girls who live in housing projects.

WNBA star Dawn Staley began a foundation to help the kids in her North Philadelphia neighborhood. It provides scholarships, basketball clinics, and after-school programs. Staley grew up in housing projects and was the first in her family to graduate from college. She has developed a personal motto: "You have to do what you don't want to do to get what you want." Staley believes that each decision lays the foundation for the next one, and that's the way she gets closer to her goals.

In recent years, a national program called Midnight Basketball, originally designed for at-risk young men, has develped teams for young women. Yvonne Pointer, director of a youth-at-risk program in Cleveland, organized such a league after girls and women asked her to. The city's division of recreation, with the help of the WNBA Cleveland Rockers, Nike, and other sponsors, opened the program for women 18 and older and six teams were formed. In addition to the basketball program, mandatory workshops help the young women understand the importance of education and sports in increasing self-esteem.

In 1996, the National Women's Sailing Association began a program called "AdventureSail" to enhance the lives of America's young people through sailing. More than 100 inner-city girls participated the first year, and more than 600 girls and boys took part during the following year. The organization's goal is to introduce sailing to 10,000 inner-city teens.

As president and founder of WomenSport International and member of the Olympic Committee, Carole Oglesby is promoting women's sports around the world. "There are 26 countries with no women in the Olympics," she said. Most are Muslim countries where women are controlled by men. According to the Iranian Olympic Committee, approximately two million women in Iran now play sports, up from 400,000 two years ago and up from only 10,000 in 1977. The women play with their bodies covered from head to toe. Some who play indoor basketball can wear shorts, but no men are allowed into the gym, and no photographs are permitted.

Within her own organization Oglesby finds disagreement on exactly what to do about this. Some members believe countries that do not allow women to compete in sports should be banned from the Olympics. Others (a majority) believe they should be allowed to compete in any sport where they will allow their women to compete, even if the women are covered from head to toe.

The Women's Sports Foundation sees the international picture changing gradually through the power of television, the Internet, and other global communications. The images of achievements of female athletes on a global scale will put considerable pressure to change on societies currently suppressing interest and limiting participation of girls and women in sports.

The ability of women of means to avoid gender discrimination in sports and to become Olympic champions supports the possibility that even nations that disapprove of female participation in sports will rally around an Olympic champion. At such historic moments, national pride supercedes the conflict of gender and sometimes religion. For example, an athletic daughter of a ruling family made the establishment of the Muslim Women's Games possible.

ROLE MODELS OF TRANSFORMATION

Boys grow up with a sense of "owning" sports. Today's female athletes are committed to letting little girls know that they, too, share that ownership.

All of the WNBA teams take seriously their position as role models. Before games begin, there is a ceremonial ball exchange with young girls from the community. Some teams have kids' clubs and special events for girls at halftime. The Women's Sports Foundation raises money for tickets for girls in WNBA cities to attend games through their "Take a Girl to a Game" program. After games there is time for autograph sessions and opportunities for girls to meet and learn about their teams and players. The audience at WNBA games is always filled with girls (and usually their moms and dads and brothers).

Kelly Kennedy said her USPV team members always sign autographs and volleyballs after their games. They also visit elementary schools and talk with boys and girls about their sport. Visits like this were never on the agenda when she was in grade school, Kennedy said. She also finds that little boys are just as excited to meet athletic women as the girls are, and high school kids often come over to the elementary schools to see them.

The Chicago Ice also encourages girls to get to know ice hockey. In 1999 they hosted an outing in honor of National Women and Girls in Sports Day, in conjunction with A Sporting Chance Foundation, which encourages girls to participate in sports as a means to develop life skills that lead to self-esteem, responsibility, good body image, and academic achievements. They brought approximately 40 girls to Johnny's Ice House, where the girls visited both the Chicago and St. Louis locker rooms before game time. Players from both teams answered questions and explained the game of hockey to them. The girls cheered and yelled for the Ice during the game, but both teams came away with something more important: the opportunity to meet and interact with some wonderful girls who are the future of women's sports.

Most of the women volleyball players Elaina Oden coaches at Indiana University are there with the help of scholarships, and they get the word out to girls encouraging a love of the sport. Laura Dewitz, 21, said, "We go to Indiana University sporting events together, we hold autograph sessions after games, we volunteer teaching kids to play volleyball [through Hoosier Hitters]."

Across the country hundreds of high school and college women apply for and turn out for WNBA team tryouts whenever they are held. Team managers say they are constantly answering phone inquiries from these young women, too.

Scores of television commercials during broadcasts of women's team games are all about role modeling. The popular WNBA television ads during the 1998 season feature a group of young girls giving some attitude to the players and implying that the younger generation is counting on them. There are also many public service TV ads by companies such as Reebok and Nike that encourage girls to get involved in team sports.

Television commercials heralding the approach of the National Women's Football League, the National Women's Hockey League, and Women's Major League Baseball show young girls in a huddle planning strategy. The theme is, "It's just a matter of time."

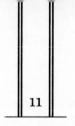

11

WHO NEEDS TESTOSTERONE?

~

"We're women who like to knock people's heads off,
and then put on a skirt and go dance."

—Brandi Chastain, U.S. Women's National Soccer Team

C HICAGO ICE TEAM MEMBER Marcy Bright used to think it was testosterone that fueled the fights among men in National Hockey League games. When she got punched and knocked down in a women's game in Chicago, she changed her mind.

"I was chasing the player with the puck," said Bright, "and as I reached out from behind her with one arm to try to poke the puck away, she held my left arm and my stick underneath her left arm so that I couldn't move. I was practically on top of her back!" The player continued to hold onto Bright, even after she had passed the puck across more than half of the length of the ice! Growing tired of the dance, Bright used her right arm to reach around the player's head and throw her "forward and off of me. She didn't fall, but she put on a good act," Bright recalled.

"This, of course, stopped play because the ref only saw what I did and there is no body checking in women's hockey." On her way to the penalty box, Bright was suddenly blindsided by a fist—her first punch to the face—and an elbow to the back of the head. "I was knocked down, but as I got up to go after her, some of my teammates held me back. This almost produced an out-and-out brawl, but what really happened, as the referee was escorting the instigator off of the ice to the locker room, one of her teammates punched the ref in the chest, adding to the chaos!

"Fights are pretty rare in women's hockey," according to Bright. "It's not supposed to be part of the game," which is one of finesse because there's no checking allowed. "I once told a [male] friend of mine, who now plays for the Calgary Flames, that I didn't understand why the guys fight in NHL games. I argued that too much testosterone was their problem. But then after I started playing hockey, I realized that it's mostly adrenaline and competitiveness that fuel the aggression. He said that was 100 percent true."

Bright said aggression will ignite in games against a few of her team's arch rivals. "They are very physical, intense games."

HORMONES 'R' US! (OR NOT)

Men produce testosterone and women produce estrogen—and testosterone. So both sexes produce testosterone, but men, naturally, produce more, because they produce it in more than one set of glands. Women produce testosterone only in the adrenal glands. The amount produced varies from person to person, but men produce much more than women.

Levels of testosterone have been linked to aggression in both males and females. Men who have more testosterone than the average male are allegedly more aggressive than the average male. Ditto for women. What is the average? We don't really know. Most scientists still believe men have a natural or hardwired predisposition to aggression. However, in humans, socialization, culture, and the ability to think mitigate this influence. Never mind testes or breasts, penises or vaginas. The brain is the big organ, and it is still in control. Therefore, all testosterone does is give men a bit of an advantage in sheer physical force because it helps build larger muscle mass, but if they don't use it, they lose it, too.

Women don't need testosterone for strong muscles either, despite what many people believe. In fact, estrogen may give us an added benefit of pain reduction. (Why else would any woman go through childbirth more than once?) Our muscles can be just as strong as men's. Because men have more testosterone, they have more muscle mass and more red cells in their blood plasma. This makes building muscles easier for them. Women have to work harder, but that's the only difference. And this subtlety should not be lost on any of us, because in the struggle for equality, we have always had to work harder—just to prove we can do it. But women have endless capacity and are tough in other ways.

THE CULTURAL MESSAGE IS STRONGER
THAN HORMONES

"Your hormones don't make you anything," according to Natalie Angier's 1998 book *Woman: An Intimate Geography.* "Habit and circumstance can have a more profound effect on behavior than anything hormonal. A person who is accustomed to deference will be obeyed into old age, whatever her or his estrogen or testosterone or androstenedione levels may be doing or failing to do." Angier gives this example: "A tomcat that sprayed your house with territorial and reproductive resolve before being neutered may well continue spraying when his testicles are gone. He has learned how to do it and though the impetus to start spraying may have come with a pubertal surge in testosterone, he no longer needs the hormone to know, as cats know, for they are infinitely wise, that a tomcat must leave a spackle of pong wherever he goes."

Angier makes a strong case that "despite society's belief to the contrary, women are by nature aggressive creatures." Until age three, there is no difference in the expression of aggression. Without language, we use our bodies. It's only after three that the effects of socialization—which begin at birth—take over. Girls are protected, taught to play with dolls, play house, and take care of people. They learn to submerge their natural aggression into indirect aggression.

"One reason we may never settle the nature-nurture debate of male-female differences is that parents begin interacting differently from birth depending on the sex of the child," said Joni Johnston, a clinical psychologist, columnist for *Woman's World* magazine, and author of *The Complete Idiot's Guide to Psychology*. "We focus on different behaviors and we interpret the same behavior differently. If you follow traditional thinking, you are much more likely to believe your bawling six-month-old boy is angry but your squalling six-month-old daughter is sad or afraid. Such gender imprinting shapes our identities from birth."

Johnston points to the birth control pill as the impetus for change in traditional gender roles. "Women were freed to choose the number of children they had, and therefore could enter the workforce in greater numbers. Voila! They got in touch with their 'masculine side,' and proved that sex roles could be transformed."

According to Johnston, "Your gender identity is much more complicated than your sexual identity—it's your total pattern of traits, tastes, and interests. In the past, masculinity and femininity were thought to be polar opposites (pink or blue, passive or aggressive).

Men were thought to have instrumental qualities (to take action) and women were believed to have expressive qualities (nurturant, gentleness). There were often dire consequences for failing to conform to these gender norms.

"Gender is a fundamental part of your self-concept. From birth, a boy and a girl will have dramatically different experience—just because they are of different sexes. And gender does more than shape who we are. It can have a profound influence on what we, and others, think we're worth. Luckily, gender identity is much more complicated than mere biological sex. And it's this fact that can even the odds for women," Johnston believes.

ARE WE FREE TO BE AGGRESSIVE?

We are physically and emotionally able to be aggressive, yet women still have to be careful how they use it. In the workplace, women are learning to be *assertive*. It's OK to assert yourself, we are told, so you are not perceived as a doormat, but can you be aggressive? Aggression is still perceived as not nice by men and some women. We can compete with other women to be Miss America, and we can get aggressive shopping for bargains (with other women because everybody knows men hate shopping—think about that stereotype!). We can be aggressive over a man, and, sadly, this is where some women do exert their aggression, fighting with other women over the "prize."

"The word *aggressive* has a negative connotation for most women," writes Adrienne Mendell in her book, *How Men Think*. "As a therapist, I used to encourage women to be assertive not aggressive. But not anymore. I have come to realize there are positive as well as negative aspects of aggression. Aggressive can mean hostile or contentious, but it can also mean forceful, determined, forward, and bold. I am not going to encourage you to be hostile or contentious. These behaviors will get you nowhere. But I am going to encourage you to be forceful, determined, forward, and bold."

Until now, women have never had an acceptable outlet for aggression, so it was often diverted into manipulation or depression. Instead of learning how to bat a ball, we learned how to bat our eyelashes. In story after story from women playing team sports, we hear about the satisfaction that comes from smashing baseballs and hockey pucks with all their might, from chasing and kicking the soccer ball and fighting off the opponents. Women are thrilled at discovering their innate aggression.

Carrie Matczynski, a Chicago Ice hockey player, said her family loves to come and watch women being aggressive. Some people are puzzled by this. There's a belief that aggressive instincts cannot be "in the blood" of women, that testosterone is the fuel of athletic competition and women athletes must, therefore, be manly. Or, people think that it is unfeminine to be competitive. A man sitting in the bleachers watching his daughter's basketball game remarked that one of the players was not aggressive enough. "You have to teach girls to be aggressive," he said. Is that true? Is aggression foreign to us?

When asked for her take on the nature vs. nurture theme in women's team sports, that is, the idea that women are not naturally aggressive, sports psychologist Carole Oglesby pointed to the rapid change in women's sports and said, "My gut reaction is they won't say this much longer." She said, "Human nature is incredibly malleable. It is not a rigid formation from birth. That women are not naturally aggressive is a gross simplification. Aggressivity has been carefully taught out of girls. We probably do have to teach girls at first."

Freud also pointed out that aggression (along with sex) is one of the basic human drives. But Freud was never too sure of himself with women.

In sports, an equal number of boys and girls play together on junior teams. But when they become teenagers, the rules change and they play on separate but allegedly "equal" teams. The girls' basketball court is smaller, and so is the ball. The hardball becomes a softball. There is the silent message that girls are more delicate than boys. Does aggression in kids go away when estrogen appears? If so, then how do we explain all the strong women in this book—some small, some tall, some muscular?

DO WE NEED TO COMPETE OR COOPERATE?

But open aggression on the sporting field? Can we let it loose? In fact, if we don't play aggressively, we are accused of playing like a girl, God forbid. And apparently more and more girls and women are letting it loose.

"The sports with the most sustained growth were the sweaty, grunty, and aggressive sports. That tells me that there is a sense of self-confidence among women today. They can participate in sports that bring them joy and society doesn't insist that they can't show aggressiveness or assertiveness," said Linda Jean Carpenter in the *New York Times* in May 2000. Carpenter and R. Vivian Acosta report every two years on the progress of Title IX compliance.

Most women in this book relate to an aggressive side.

"I need to compete. It is in my blood," said Kim Many, who plays basketball in a recreational league. "I love to compete. Team sports are the best way to do this. I have always related to my athletic side and prowess more so than my brain," said Many. "Playing sports is the most obvious thing, which proves that a positive mental attitude can increase your performance. Believing in yourself and your abilities has direct positive results on the court."

"I'm amazed how competitive all the teams are," Mary McNichol said of her suburban soccer league of women in their 30s and 40s.

"We really get tough on the field." She was proud the day when her team got collectively tough and beat younger trash-talking opponents.

Katie Kauffman, a member of the U.S. Women's National Field Hockey Team, has made playing competitive field hockey a priority in her life because of "the thrill of playing and competing and getting to tournaments like the World Cup and Olympic Games. I just love to compete, and that is what gets me out of bed every day to train." Kauffman said she wasn't particularly athletic as a child. "I liked my Barbies and going to the pool." She admitted to sometimes running around the track at the high school where her dad was a coach. Two of Kauffman's three sisters played field hockey in college.

Kathleen Connolly said a girl's soccer game she attended with her four-year-old daughter "was so competitive I couldn't pull myself away." She said it was better than the softball tournament in which she had just finished playing. "Someone asked me if it bothered me that girls are so tough. Does it look like it bothers me?" Connolly was still wearing sports clothes and cleats.

The Melpomene Institute is conducting a survey to learn more about girls' and boys' attitudes about competition. Now that so many girls are involved in sports, they believe there are issues to look at. Although the primary reason for both sexes to play sports is to have fun, the role of competition as a motivator is not clear, especially for girls. The study addresses motivation for participation in the team as well as attitudes toward competition and coaching methods that are most successful.

From childhood, girls are trained to be cooperative and build relationships. They are not raised to compete, and sometimes these opposing ideas get in the way of the game.

"Sometimes winning becomes tough when you have friends on the opposing team," said Marcy Bright of the Chicago Ice. Mary

Gutowski also found this true. Building the high-level competitive team she dreamed of was a struggle because some players would rather just play with friends. "It's quite an issue," she admits, "playing with friends or being competitive. Anytime you get 45 women together, you are going to have differences of opinion," Gutowski said.

Bright told of "one time we bumped a team out of the play-offs after being down three goals to none in the second period. We came back and won, five to four. I certainly feel bad for my friends who lost, but there's nothing better than winning a championship and holding that trophy over your head, knowing what it took to get there. Knowing that we'd never be there without teamwork, communication, confidence, aggressiveness, persistence, and coaches who believe in us."

Angier put it best in her wonderful book:

"The problem of ignoring female aggression is that we who are aggressive, we girls and women and obligate primates, feel confused, as though something is missing in the equation, the interpretation of self and impulse. We're left to wander through the thickets of our profound ferocity, our roaring hungers and drives, and we're tossed in the playground to thrash it out among ourselves, girl to girl, knowing that we must prove ourselves and negotiate and strut and calibrate but seeing scant evidence of the struggle onscreen or in books or on biology's docket. We are left feeling like 'error variants,' in the words of one female scientist, wondering why we aren't nicer than we are, and why we want so much, and why we can't sit still."

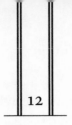

12

BEING STRONG

~

"I don't know if physical strength can enhance those other, intangible strengths, if a better-braced body can give one ovarios of heart. It's a good gimmick, though, a place to start, or to return to when all else fails. The body will be there to do its bit, to take another crack at life, and to propel you forward, suitcase in hand, not on wheels."

—FROM WOMAN: AN INTIMATE GEOGRAPHY, BY NATALIE ANGIER

WHEN ROWER VIRGINIA AMOS did her first workouts on the erg machines in the boathouse, she said she thought she would die. And when Mavis Albin played her first game of basketball after 40 years, it took her two weeks to recuperate. But both Amos and Albin were motivated by a desire to play and worked hard at becoming strong again. Now Amos "feels lousy" if she doesn't get her workout or rowing, and Albin can play as many as four games a day without tiring.

There used to be a medical belief that if women did any exercise their wombs would drop. Victorian ladies carried handkerchiefs so they could sniff smelling salts in case they got the vapors from something strenuous—physical or mental.

The argument that women are the weaker sex in anything physical has always been without merit. We have always done the grunt work, schlepping the water from the well, tilling the fields, carrying our babies on our backs. Yet for decades, doctors discouraged women from participating in sports because, in addition to making the uterus drop, it was believed that women, being smaller and weaker, would get hurt. (In reality, we are not that much smaller than men, and between the ages of 6 and 11, on average, girls are actually bigger and rougher than boys.)

Some theorized in the past that too much physical activity made a woman's menstrual period cease. And while this can happen, exercise is not to blame. It happens when excessive weight loss goes with it. Then there is no more fuel to care for the system. A phenomenon called the "athletic triad" is the combination of excessive athletic activity, weight loss, and menstrual abnormalities. When the estrogen level drops, causing menstruation to stop, it leads to the loss of bone density.

Those theories that women will be damaged by athlete participation have been thrown off the court, but fears linger. Seeing us running full speed and crashing into another player or getting jabbed in the eye or breast with a flying elbow still evokes negative responses from those around us. The cultural myth is that boys are expected to get battered on the playing field. (It will make a man of him.) When it happens to a girl, people ask why was she there in the first place. When the mature female athletes of the Louisiana Tigerettes Hi-Tops played a basketball exhibition during the Houston Comets' halftime, they heard a few people comment that they shouldn't be playing because they could get hurt. Why? Because they were over 50, or because they were women? Were they facing double discrimination?

Loretta Hill, 60, of Baton Rouge, joined the Louisiana Tigerettes Hi-Tops in 2000 because she needed more sports activity in her life.

She played basketball and softball in college in Lafayette, Louisiana. After retirement from supervising inside sales for an instrumentation company in the petrochemical industry, she signed up with a Baton Rouge recreational league to play softball. She played twice in the National Senior Games and also played tennis in the nationals. She has always played coed softball and works out with weights. Hill, a widow, said that with the Louisiana Hi-Tops basketball team, "We're always doing something different, like scrimmaging with the guys at the Y. They give us a good workout," she said, "and are always surprised at the challenge.

"I retired to do all the fun things," said Hill. "I like to get a cup of coffee, sit on my patio, and think what I'll do today. This morning I played tennis, came home and changed, and went out to lunch with a friend. The more I do, the more up I am." She keeps two bikes in the house so she can go for a ride anytime and with anyone. She keeps a rowing machine, StairMaster, and other exercise equipment at home. She used to run and play racquetball with her son until he moved to another city. "It gives you a lot more energy," Hill said. "If I miss a day, I feel sluggish." Hill's 12-year-old grandson came to her softball game recently, and she hit a home run. "That's my nana," he said. "Look at her run."

CHANGING THE PHYSICAL PATTERNS

Despite all the attention to healthful physical activity in recent years, it is not as widespread as it appears. After graduation from high schools and colleges, most women settle into an existence characterized by a domestic or domestic-and-job pattern, one that does not include regular, self-motivated recreational exercise. Many women with access to health clubs continue some kind of workout, but for the majority of women who are poor or who get pregnant early, exercise is not part of their lifestyle. Physical fitness or unfitness patterns that have become established during the young-adult life cycle tend to persist, unfortunately, to be further modified downward after menopause.

Regular physical activity is associated with numerous health benefits, including lower incidences of cardiovascular disease, diabetes, osteoporosis, and osteoarthritis. In addition, exercise causes the brain to release substances that elevate our mood (not just testosterone and adrenaline). These substances, called endorphins, have a well-documented, beneficial effect on a person's sense of well-being, contributing to a noticeable decrease in both depression and anxiety.

A study of women runners gave evidence that with the increasing numbers of miles run, there was a corresponding higher ratio of the "good" cholesterol (HDL) in the blood, compared with the "bad" (LDL). Obviously, the prescribed amount of exercise varies with age and with the choice of the goal. Younger women who wish to improve their cardiopulmonary fitness need an intense regimen, working up sweat with at least 20 minutes of aerobic exercise three times a week. (Sounds like a soccer game.)

A personal trainer recently told a reporter that getting exercise is the only thing about our health we negotiate. We never negotiate whether or not we'll brush our teeth today. Nevertheless, if you don't have to answer to anyone, it is easier to make excuses or put off exercise. But that is changing. It's not easy to make excuses if you are part of a team because if you do, you let the team down. For example, rowers cannot take out the boat unless everyone is there. Overwhelmingly, women involved in team sports say they never miss a practice or a game.

CONDITION, CONDITION, CONDITION

Our muscles are just sitting there waiting to be used. They really can get strong at any age and any time we want them to. At 20 or 50 or 80, a few months of conditioning can make them strong again. Those muscle spasms and aches occur after the first exercise of the season, but gradually the muscles acclimate. Muscle protects our bones, so if our muscles are strong, our bones are less vulnerable to breakage. However, if we don't keep our muscles in condition, they lose out in the battle with fat as we age.

We go back to that early cultural conditioning. Men assume they are strong; women have to prove it. But we can get strong anytime we want to. Our muscles are designed to work hard, and they do this by contracting (shortening) or relaxing (lengthening).

In real estate the three most important considerations are location, location, location. In sports, these are condition, condition, condition. Flexibility, strength, endurance, and coordination are the goals of conditioning according to most sports trainers and physical therapists. Flexibility, which is often overlooked, is improved with routine stretching. Weight training creates strength. Cardiovascular endurance is built up with anaerobic and aerobic conditioning. And developing particular skills brings good coordination.

According to Dr. Timothy Hewett, director of research at the Cincinnati Sportsmedicine and Orthopaedic Center, "Professional athletes spend more time in the weight and conditioning room than on the court. However, amateurs [except the rowers] probably do not."

"Conditioning is extremely important for all women prior to participation in sports," said Jo Hannafin, M.D., founder and codirector of the Women's Sports Medicine Center at the Hospital for

Special Surgery in New York and U.S. Rowing Team physician. She said this is important, "particularly in team sports when the participants have a long history of competition. If athletes of any gender want to participate at a competitive, aggressive level, they must maintain their level of fitness and conditioning or they are at increased risk of injury.

"If a woman begins an 'on-water' rowing program," Hannafin said, "the appropriate strength will generally develop as technique develops. If someone begins an aggressive ergometer 'on-land' training program (like the ones designed similar to spinning programs for cycling in gyms), the risk of injury is possibly greater if the individual doesn't have good strength of the back and abdominal musculature or has poor technique. It is important to develop a sound base of good technique prior to training with high intensity . . . but this is true for just about any sport."

In the case of rowing, Hannafin believes that doing the sport is a better way to get into conditioning because you learn the stroke mechanics before you knock yourself out on the erg machines.

"Rowing is a wonderful sport for women with and without sports experience," Hannafin said. "The important thing is to learn proper stroke mechanics whether you are training on a rowing ergometer or rowing in a boat. It provides fantastic cardiovascular exercise and is often suitable for women who have sustained knee injuries that make running, soccer, and basketball difficult to do. The most common injuries seen in rowing are overuse injuries to the patella [kneecap], shoulder, and low back."

THE SPORTS MOST LIKELY TO INJURE YOU

Hannafin said basketball and soccer continue to generate the most injuries in women's team sports. (In nonteam sports, skiing, running, and tennis lead her list.) She said she sees a mix of high school, college, and postcollegiate athletes with "the majority being women who are postcollege, nonelite athletes." She said women in their 30s, 40s, and 50s who come in with injuries have a strong desire to return to their sport or gym activities.

"Since we started the Women's Sports Medicine Center, we have attracted a following of women who very much want to continue to be active and who don't want to be told to stop the activities they love," said Hannafin.

There are no long-term studies yet of sports-related injuries to adult women, but there are some of organized sports at the college and high school levels. The National Athletic Trainers' Association (NATA) did a three-year study of injuries in high school sports. During the study of 250 schools, 23,566 injuries occurred, and an average of 6,000 students were injured at least once each year. Football had the highest rate of injury and volleyball the lowest. The largest proportion of fractures came from boys' baseball, basketball, soccer, and softball.

Here are some of the things they discovered about girls' sports:

- Most injuries occurred during practice rather than the game, except for soccer, which was the only sport with a larger proportion of injuries in games than practice (for both men and women).

- The highest frequency of knee injury appeared in girls' soccer (19.4 percent), while baseball had the lowest with 10.5 percent.

- The largest portion of surgeries among the 10 sports was for girls' basketball and the lowest was field hockey.

- Of injuries requiring surgery, 60.3 percent were to the knee.

- Field hockey was the only sport where sprains and strains accounted for less than 50 percent of the total injuries.

THE FEMALE ACHILLES' HEEL IS THE KNEE

The knee is the workhorse joint. It carries our weight and handles most of the wear and tear of walking, running, jumping, dancing, and all that we do in an upright position. Sudden twisting motions can damage the knees, but there are many other reasons for damage to the knees; falls, osteoarthritis, or simply years of wear and tear— especially from being overweight. Knees rely on ligaments for support. These tough bands of tissue connect bones and cartilage. Strong ligaments give the knee stability and limit side-to-side motion. Two ligaments crossing the middle of the knee restrain front to back movement and provide stability when the knee pivots. Damage to any of these structures can be serious. Cartilage cannot regenerate, and ligaments are very slow to heal.

Ligaments are stretched or torn if the knee is twisted. The most commonly injured are the medial collateral ligament along the inner knee and the anterior cruciate ligament (ACL) in the center of the knee. ACL damage can result in chronic knee instability. It can be reconstructed surgically by taking a tendon from other sites around the knee and creating a new ACL. However, recovery is a long and arduous process that may involve months on crutches and even longer in physical therapy, as recreational basketball player Elizabeth McCarthy learned. McCarthy had a partial tear in her ACL, which required physical therapy; then another injury resulted in a full tear, meaning surgery and lots more physical therapy.

"I have to live with the fact that I must spend three days a week in the gym doing hamstring and quadriceps exercises. Not a lot, but if I cheat, I feel it. It is always tempting to think that I don't need to do it if I have been playing a lot, but it will start to hurt and it is not worth putting my knees at risk. I guess basketball is worth the risk to me since it is an integral part of my day-to-day life, not just a few weekends a year."

Whatever the reason, knee injuries are a serious problem for women—three or more times more serious than for men—especially the infamous ACL. Rebecca Lobo tore her ACL a few seconds into the first game of the New York Liberty season in 1999. She was unable to play in that season or in 2000.

The American Orthopaedic Society for Sports Medicine estimates that 10,000 women experience debilitating knee injuries every year at the college level. At the high school level, the number rises to 20,000. Pivoting and jumping are moves that put the knee at risk, and these moves are common in soccer, basketball, and volleyball.

According to the National Collegiate Athletic Association, women playing soccer and basketball suffer three to five times as many ACL injuries as men. Other authorities believe the figure is more like five to eight times more common in women. While no one has a definitive reason women are affected more than men, the theories are that causes are anatomical and possibly hormonal. The narrowness of the notch in a woman's knee where the ligament is attached may limit flexibility. Also, estrogen may make a woman's ligaments looser. A third theory is that because our muscle mass is not the same size as a man's, the muscles around the knee do not protect us as well. In general women have longer legs and shorter torsos, which gives us a lower center of gravity and less muscle mass. Women also tend to run, jump, and land in a more upright position.

However, some believe the higher number of injuries result because women don't learn to use certain muscles when jumping and pivoting the same way men do. Women tend to rely on their quadriceps while men depend more on their hamstrings. The quadriceps muscle (in front of the thigh) straightens the knee. The hamstring muscle (in back of the thigh) bends the knee and is more protective of the ACL.

Dr. Frank Noyes, director of the Cincinnati Sportsmedicine Research and Education Foundation, believes training can reduce the disparity in men's and women's knee injuries. He has developed a jump-training program and conditioning program called Cincinnati Sportsmetrics, which is being adopted in hundreds of high schools and colleges and is available on videotape.

"Through sophisticated tests and measurements, we can evaluate an athlete's strength, coordination, and body alignment," claimed Noyes on the Cincinnati Sportsmedicine Research and Education Foundation website. "These factors, we hope, will help us identify those athletes who are at risk, especially female athletes. The goal is to reach kids before they begin competitive sports and offer a training program that might decrease their risk of developing knee injuries."

POWERFUL MEDICINE

All the women in this book have been injured to some degree playing their sport, but none let it keep them away from the game. Bumps, bruises, and sprains go with the territory. But rather than think of sports as physical risk, they think of it as powerful medicine. As Mavis Albin said of her basketball team of 50- and 60-somethings, "We pad everything; we brace everything." Some women (of all ages) take painkillers like ibuprofen or arthritis medications ahead of time to blunt the pain. Soccer player Gail Lipstein didn't let breast cancer prevent her from playing the game she loved. Other women have played through cancer, too.

In the spring of 1996, Elizabeth McCarthy, then 27, sprained her ankle while on a ski jump. When her leg was x-rayed doctors found a tumor on her shin. At first they did not think it was cancer, but further tests revealed the tumor was growing, and they found others. This rare bone malignancy, more common to women than to men, required nearly eight months of chemotherapy and radiation. Then in the summer of 1999, another tumor was found, and McCarthy went through five more months of treatment.

At first people felt she should not push her body so much, but the consensus of her doctors was that if she wanted to do something life-affirming like play sports, then she should do it. Her orthopedic doctor, McCarthy said, is extremely aggressive.

"I think it has helped my self-image in the sense that I feel young and strong when I am playing. That is much preferable to feeling achy and sick from all the medical treatments I have received. Thursday night I played in back-to-back games and never took a break, and it made me feel very vibrant and healthy. When I talk to other people going through radiation or chemotherapy I don't think that many of them have an outlet like this, and it makes the disease more powerful. Basketball makes me feel powerful."

REAL MEN MARRY ATHLETES

~

"We're best friends, and we're always going to be best friends.
He's my boyfriend, yeah, but he's my support system."

—HIGH SCHOOL BASKETBALL PLAYER REBECCA RICHMAN TO REPORTER
ANDREW FRIEDMAN, *NEW YORK TIMES*, OCTOBER 2000

FILMMAKER GINA PRINCE-BYTHEWOOD made *Love and Basket-ball*, a movie released in 2000, because she wanted to show that a woman can be an aggressive athlete and still be feminine. Judging by the fine reviews and ticket sales, this is a story that needed to be told. And Prince-Bythewood, a basketball and track athlete herself, was the one to tell it. The movie presents a very moving portrait of the pressures a young woman faces when she loves to play basketball and loves a man, too.

The movie's protagonist, Monica, at age 11 moves to a new neighborhood, next door to Quincy, whose dad is grooming him to follow his footsteps into the NBA. At first, Quincy is put off by the discovery that a "mere girl" can play as well as he can, but they become best friends. As they get older, even though it's pretty obvious they do love each other, the friendship does not become romantic. Monica is too involved in basketball to understand the flirtation and dress code that come so naturally to teenaged girls who are pursuing Quincy. Monica doesn't give Quincy that kind of attention, although she seems to be angry at him when he responds to the other girls.

Monica's older sister fixes her up with a blind date and dresses her up. Quincy notices that his best friend is pretty hot. This leads to romance, but it is not a lasting one until they learn how to break away from stereotype and balance love and basketball. The movie is deeply felt, a terrific love story, and a wise look at what it takes to make love work.

Although Prince-Bythewood would not admit the love story is from her own life, much of the background is similar. Prince-Bythewood, who is 30, grew up in Pacific Grove, California, with two older sisters and a younger brother. Their mom put them in a soccer league—they were the only girls in the league in the 1970s—and they played all seasonal sports with boys.

She said, "The girls just sat around, but after we played others joined in. I always loved sports, so it wasn't strange to me." Prince-Bythewood played every sport all the way through school but focused primarily on basketball. "I don't know what it is about being part of a team," she said. "I loved the team. With a team your emotions are so high or so low—and they can change from high to low in an instant. There's a bond. I lived for games," she said.

"My dad loved bragging about me. He was the loudest one in the stands," Prince-Bythewood said. Although her mom came to games, she would read a book. It bothered Prince-Bythewood that their games were earlier than the boys' games, scheduled at a time when few people would come. In her senior high school year, Prince-Bythewood was recruited by a few colleges, but she had her heart set on going to UCLA, so she tried out for the team when she got there.

"It was the first time I was up against women over six feet," said Prince-Bythewood, who is five feet eight. "My first shot got blocked, and it killed my confidence. It was always a big regret that I let my fear prevent me from getting what I wanted. I've been playing since the age of six, and I really miss it. I so miss the team, the locker room, riding the buses, hearing the nickname of 'Witch Hazel' [because she used it on her skin]. Sports is a special community."

Because Prince-Bythewood missed the boat on basketball at UCLA, she tried out for track. She worked the track five hours a day, and the team won several championships. "It was my best year in college," she said. By junior year it was time for film school, and Prince-Bythewood knew she needed total devotion for that or track—she couldn't do both. Meanwhile, Bill Cosby had come to a track meet and made an introduction that got her a film job, and that led to her career, which allowed her by age 30 to have written and directed her first major movie, produced by Spike Lee and New Line Cinema.

"I believe everything happens for a reason," she said. "The movie was a catharsis for me." While making the movie, Prince-Bythewood worked with the WNBA Los Angeles Sparks assistant coach who was an advisor to the film. "I was watching the players every day," Prince-Bythewood said. "Once they put on the uniform, they become that team. It's such an amazing thing. I was so hyped about playing, I wanted to jump into the game." Occasionally, she did get onto the court, and the coach told her she could have played at UCLA.

"Damn," the filmmaker said, "look what I missed!"

Prince-Bythewood is getting her chance to play basketball again, however. The Sparks coach is setting up an AAU (Amateur Athletic Union) team and has invited Prince-Bythewood to play. "It just excites me," she said.

Prince-Bythewood's movie really showed the social pressures on female athletes who are also interested in romance, a problem that continues. Men may not understand for a while. In fact, one of the movie's reviewers, Elvis Mitchell of the *New York Times*, praised Prince-Bythewood's talent and enjoyed the movie, but he wrote, "It's not really about anything."

SEXUALITY AND SPORTS

Perhaps that movie reviewer didn't get it. The movie was very much about attitude and social rules girls and women have been struggling with for years. Many girls dropped out of sports or would not get involved because boys would not approach them for dates, assuming they were gay.

"If you were a woman athlete, you almost had to be gay," said Diana Nyad, an Olympic athlete and lesbian, speaking in 1999 at a program called "Breaking the Silence: Gays and Lesbians in Professional Sports." It was a landmark event that was sponsored by the *New York Times*. Trying to explain the pervasive homophobia, Nyad said, "Women were not supposed to be athletic. Therefore, if they were, they must be gay." Many women avoided sports because of this, but Nyad said, "I think most women today in sports are hetero."

"If you were a woman and an athlete, you were probably called a lesbian," Mariah Burton Nelson told the audience. "The first athletes were lesbians, because no other women would push the envelope. Female athletes are threatening; we're pushing the frontier," she said. "Brave lesbian pioneers opened the doors." Burton Nelson, who played basketball in college and professionally, said the media always questioned her, "Don't your boyfriends resent it? How can you be a woman and a basketball player? Today," she said, "those same media people will say, 'Why don't you come out?'" Burton Nelson is a psychologist and the author of *The Stronger Women Get, the More Men Love Football* and two other books about women in sports.

"In those days [the early 1970s] you were labeled gay if you were interested in sports," Sue Nesbihal recalled. "I didn't care because I loved sports. But after college it bothered me. Everyone assumed I must be gay. We had to brave that attitude." But Nesbihal, like many others, persisted with sports. "Luckily, I met a man who encouraged me." She said her husband and later her son came to her softball games when she played in an industrial league. Now her son, 15, who comes to her track meets and helps sell T-shirts, is supportive.

"The WNBA is lesbian and straight and they socialize together," Nyad said, "yet the coaches and owners still don't talk about it." Nyad attributes this to two reasons: First, it is a personal subject. Second, there are financial considerations because, admittedly, coming out will upset the sponsors. Nyad talked about image control. The sponsors say, "You're all great, but if you can, mention husbands, boyfriends." She said there are better job opportunities and media coverage for heterosexual women. For example, Suzie McConnell Serio, who retired from the Cleveland Rockers in 2000, and Sheryl Swoopes, of the Houston Comets, get lots of media play because they are mothers. Ironically, this doesn't mean they are heterosexual because gays are parents, too, but the media love to play up their motherhood.

Of course, it is also of great importance to see mothers play at the top of their games. It's not just an anti-lesbian thing. Women who play are proud that their children can see their mother in the role of athlete and share this aspect of their lives. McConnell Serio recently told an interviewer that she bought one-pound weights for her kids, so when she has to work out at home, they can join her. Most children of players—and coaches—are quite visible at games. The last scene in *Love and Basketball* shows Mom on the court and Daddy in the stands holding the baby.

Yet, even though women's sports have been more accepted, there is still an overriding feeling in American society that most aggressive athletic women—or at least the ones with impressive height or muscles, or short hair—must be homosexual. They are subtly, or not so subtly, urged to present themselves in a stereotypically feminine way, with husband and children whenever possible. Some say that one of the reasons the U.S. Women's National Soccer Team was so universally embraced by fans of both sexes is that they were "babes." They did not look threatening. In other words, they did not appear too muscular, too tall, too powerful—even though they were all of those things.

While a WNBA game is known as a good "pick-up" arena for lesbians, New York Liberty fans were asked to tone down obvious lesbian overtures, like signs reading "Lesbians for Liberty" or "Another Dyke Fan." The TV cameras focus on the families. But most people don't flaunt their sexual preference either way. They just want to play—or watch—a sport they love. And they want to be able to love (either way) and play their game.

THE ROMANTIC ARENA

Like *Love and Basketball*'s Monica, Kathleen Connolly was too busy with basketball at Christ the King High School to worry about dating, but she didn't let love slip by either. Connolly is six feet tall—five inches taller than her husband—but they fell in love when she was a high school athlete and have never been apart since. "He liked that I played sports," Connolly said about what attracted Jeff Connolly.

Katie Kauffman, who is on the U.S. Women's National Field Hockey team, met her boyfriend, Keith, after she returned from the

Atlanta Olympics. Keith, who is on a soccer team, is her biggest inspiration. "He is my greatest supporter who insists I never give up to reach any dream. In fact, he comes out and plays hockey with me, and it is quite a laugh. He actually beat me at this one game we played for fun, and I was so annoyed, but I played it off quite well.

"I was definitely attracted to him, and we would run into one another in the weight room and at parties of friends. He finally asked me if he could call me and took my number. Well, he didn't call for a week, so I called him. We went on our first date. He picked me up and took me to Great Falls, which is a popular park in northern Virginia." Kauffman said, "From there on we have been together and so happy. He is so supportive and loves to come and watch me play. In fact, in 1998, he surprised me by coming over to Holland to watch me play in the World Cup. He was there the whole two weeks and lived in a tent at a local campground. It was so great to have him there. He, too, travels a lot and has played soccer in a few foreign countries. He now is in Miami and keeps urging me to pursue my dreams. We have been together for nearly three years."

Jen Stitzell's romantic life changed, too, when at the end of her first year playing hockey with the Chicago Ice, Rick Tekip joined as an assistant coach. "I was attracted to him but too shy to tell him [despite her new aggressive self-image]. I was lusting after him, but he was oblivious. I thought any man who volunteered his time to coach women had to be special," Stitzell said, "but I thought he must have a girlfriend." One of Stitzell's friends had more courage and said she would tell Tekip that Stitzell had season tickets for the Blackhawks and would like him to go to a game with her. Stitzell waited in the locker room until her friend came back and told her that Tekip accepted.

"I don't remember the game," Stitzell admitted.

"Your friends were across the rink with binoculars watching us," Tekip said. Their new relationship naturally affected their relationship on the ice, so Tekip quit coaching Stitzell's squad and now just comes to watch her games.

Unlike with Stitzell, hockey participation ended a romance for Carrie Matczynski, who has played with the Ice since 1997. She broke up with a former boyfriend over hockey. "He was never active. He never went to games. He didn't mind my jogging, but he hated the hockey." They had a big disagreement, and hockey won.

Joe Albin still adores Mavis, who is playing basketball at 63. Soccer player Gail Lipstein met her husband in college, where she was a top athlete. "He was three years ahead, and he came to help the basketball team, although he did not play sports anymore." He was always supportive and encouraged Lipstein's participation in sports.

While many women in this book have supportive men in their lives, some do not. Some husbands are not interested; some think the team sports activity is a passing fad; others don't mind as long as it doesn't interfere with their lives. And some may not be interested in sports but love their wives—and believe whatever makes their wives happy is good for them, too.

Now that there are jocks of both sexes in high schools and colleges, and the rest of life, it may be having a profound affect on romance. On the one hand, men can identify with women who finally "get it" about sports. On the other, there may be competition involved.

14

THE CHANGING BUSINESS ARENA

~

"What she's gleaned from sports as a leader of teams rather than,
for example, as a golfer, is collaboration.
Taking sole credit is anathema."

—JAN HOFFMAN, *NEW YORK TIMES* REPORTER, ABOUT
WNBA PRESIDENT VAL ACKERMAN, MAY 26, 2000

S PORTS ARE WHERE BOYS have traditionally learned about teamwork, goal setting, and other achievement-oriented behaviors, all
of which are critical skills for success in the workplace. It's nearly
impossible for boys to grow up in this country without understanding team sports. Even those who say they are not jocks have likely
played some form of team sports in their local schoolyards or in the
city streets. Men talk about sports as a natural part of their lives. If
they no longer play team sports as adults, then they continue to
identify with the games as fans.

At work men participate in yet another sports contest or battle-
field. The object of the game is to win it for the team—whether it's
beating out the opposition for a new production contract or hiring
a talented player away from another company. The idea of winning

generally plays no part in what girls learn as they grow up. In fact, girls traditionally learn not to be competitive and to avoid conflict, because relationships are more important than any game. And girls worry about hurting somebody's feelings, as expressed by some of the Chicago Ice hockey players who sometimes have problems being competitive when they are playing against their friends.

THE NOTION OF "GAME"

Surveys of women in management reveal that 80 percent of female executives at Fortune 500 companies were "tomboys," girls who probably thought it was more fun to shoot hoops with the neighborhood guys than to play house with Barbie and Ken. There are no long-term study results yet on how playing team sports affects women in management, but some experts believe women who have played team sports have a smoother ride into the corporate world. For one thing, they understand that all the metaphors peppering the language of business really mean something.

"You know how to walk into a meeting when you know how to walk onto the court," said Atlanta corporate psychologist Joy McCarthy, 57, who played team sports throughout her childhood and college years. "Your body goes through the motions when the gun goes off or the whistle blows. Once you start, you just do it." Because of her own experience playing team sports, McCarthy is aware of a big difference in counseling women in business who have not had this experience—women who only had physical education in school versus those who were involved in competitive sports. Team sports are "not just a physical activity, but a strategic one," said McCarthy, who senses that many women "don't have the notion of 'game' or how to engage in the practice of business as a sport." Consider, for example, "you win some and lose some, but you don't take it personally." It's a matter of whether you score or not. You learn to think strategically.

A female vice president of a midsize company told McCarthy how her experiences on teams in her youth have given her a lot of resiliency in the workplace. She doesn't have to be the star every time; she doesn't have to be the one who always scores. It is even OK if she tries but doesn't win. She doesn't take it as personal rejection. "What is important is that someone is scoring and that the team is winning," McCarthy said.

"Passing the ball around is about trust and support," she said. You don't have to like a person, but you need to trust that he or she will be in position on the court. It's the same in business. You don't need to trust the person to be a friend or an intimate partner. You just need to trust that the person will have the report done in time.

Mary McNichol, who is the assistant director of information systems at Thomas Jefferson University Medical Center, believes being active in team sports makes a big difference at her job. "The guys who work for me respect that I play sports," she said. "They know I'm tough." In other words, they trust that she won't let them down, that she has the toughness to stand up for her staff. McNichol also shoots hoops with them at the company gym. "One guy who played football at a southern school complimented me when he saw how tough I was."

Carrie Matczynski, 27, said she has developed more of a team attitude at work since she started playing ice hockey. In her job, she looks at investments, acquisitions, and corporate accounting. She works with the chief financial officer of the company and she works a lot of different angles to achieve her focus and goals. "I used to like to go my own way," she said. "I'd move the puck up the ice my own way. Now I find I'm more interested in working with others, practicing team plays." This new perspective translates to her work as well as in the game.

LEARNING THE UNWRITTEN RULES

In her book *How Men Think*, gender psychologist Adrienne Mendell claims it was her experience with sailboat racing that helped her understand the problems her female patients were having in business: "Curiously, I began to realize that the problems these women were having in their jobs were similar to the problems I had encountered racing my sailboat. I wondered if the same set of unwritten rules that were operative in sailboat racing were operative in business. Could these women's problems be a consequence of their ignorance of the unwritten rules of the game?

"You are expected to know two sets of rules when you play the game of business. One set of rules governs the skills of your trade. These are the skills they taught you in school, or later on the job. Women know these rules well. But there is another set of rules in effect that women don't know: the unwritten rules of the game. The rules are never mentioned, but men expect you to honor them."

McCarthy does consultation or team development by coaching executives. This leads to one-on-one talks. She asks her clients about their early experience. For example, a woman can get a sense of team from a family or from school activities, but it's not the same as a competitive experience. And, she said, academic competition is entirely different from competing in team sports.

IT'S NOT PERSONAL

According to McCarthy, personalization is key with women who have no team experience. This is something rower Cindy Powell learned from her team—when the coach yelled at her for crashing the boat, she should not take it personally. She had to get the boat and the rowers back to safety. It was not about her. It was about the team, the game.

Boys learn to hide their emotions. When they are told to "act like a man," that doesn't mean to be more masculine, it simply means hide your emotions. While a woman would tend to ask people why they hurt her feelings, a man might not even acknowledge his feelings were hurt.

"Men can argue vigorously and still be friends," McCarthy pointed out. "They see it as competition and can beat each other up verbally." She said there is a lot of teasing and joking among men in a team development setting. Boys punch each other's shoulders, and they see it as horsing around. While some women see this kind of teasing as hurtful, men say they never tease people they don't like. According to McCarthy, this type of treatment of one another carries over into business.

COMPETE WITH CAUTION

McCarthy believes women are still censured by an unwritten rule about being openly competitive. She said that men from her generation still tell her she's too competitive. She believes the younger generation more easily accepts competitive women, but not yet very deeply.

If she were starting out in business, would she be accepted as a competitive woman? Yes and no, McCarthy said. "Yes, because it is politically correct to accept competitive women. On a cognitive level younger men and women will 'talk the talk.' Older men and women are more ambivalent. But no, because on the emotional level the picture is less clear even for younger men and women. I see women being careful in how they exhibit their competitiveness. It is OK to work with the desire to be the best, but be careful how you articulate this desire. Several clients have told me it is OK for a woman to be competitive until she wins, and then she is called a bitch, a witch, too aggressive, threatening. Her success is considered luck or, even worse, not deserved. With success she may lose friends, both male and female, among her colleagues. Women don't accept other women's expression of ego," said McCarthy. This certainly is apparent in the negative responses some women coaches said they were getting from their female team players.

HELP WANTED: WOMEN WHO KNOW THE GAME

Unwritten rules or not, women are taking their team sports experience to the office—or better, to a higher court. Twenty years ago, a sports career for a woman meant teaching physical education. Today women are owners and managers of sports teams, sportswriters, coaches, agents, athletic directors (well, a few), sports medicine physicians, and psychologists. According to the Women's Sports Foundation there are more than 6 million jobs held by women in sports-related careers, a field once exclusively male.

The men's professional sports leagues are hiring women because they know women buy nearly half the products they sell. Close to 40 percent of the ticket buyers of men's professional sports are women who also watch games on TV and buy the products being advertised.

Corporations are learning that the female consumer is very different from the male consumer in shopping habits and product desires. Because of that realization, corporations are hiring women who understand the differences and can offer insight into the female perspective.

Several women in high-profile sports careers created the Women in Sports Careers Foundation (WISCF) to help other women find jobs in sports. The Women's Sports Foundation also guides women looking for sports jobs, warning that in addition to the obvious rules like working long hours and networking, we need to learn the unwritten rules that apply specifically to women who want to work in the industry. Such rules include not dating staff or players, not trying to become one of the boys and instead working hard to understand them and to be understood by them. A good sense of humor and a thick skin are other prerequisites, along with being prepared for male attitude.

Studies are in progress about women working in the management of professional sports. Once they are completed, perhaps we will know more about the rules—both written and unwritten.

NOW, SHOW US THE MONEY

Although more organizations see the value of hiring women as athletes and behind-the-scenes contributors, female professional basketball players earn a fraction of what male players earn, and the World Cup soccer team had to fight for a livable wage. Professional volleyball players accepted less money (for now) because they want the exposure that playing will bring.

As noted earlier, coaches and athletic directors for women's teams are also paid a fraction of what the men's teams get. The argument used is that women don't generate equal ratings and attendance and therefore dollars. WNBA ticket prices were purposely kept lower than NBA prices to encourage attendance. This strategy seems to have worked because the stadiums are filling, and ticket prices are likely to increase in tandem with continued and increasing attendance. Hopefully players' salaries will go up, too.

THE BEST JOB OF ALL

If you ask Kris Fillat of San Diego her occupation, she will tell you she is an athlete and has been for 10 years. As a member of the U.S. Women's National Field Hockey Team, Fillat trains, travels, and competes; when she's not doing that, she works at Home Depot. Katie Kauffman, Kelli James, and other members of the same team also have jobs at Home Depot in other cities.

"[Field hockey is] fun and what I have always done. Home Depot allows me to continue to do it this late in life," said Fillat, who grew up playing sports with two brothers and went to the University of Iowa on an athletic scholarship. She's been on the national team since 1990, played in the 1996 and 2000 Olympics, and is a medalist in other international games. Fillat lamented, "We are one of the only countries in the world whose Olympic teams are not supported by our government. It's up to companies to fund the entire United States Olympic Committee.

"If it weren't for Home Depot, I would have had to stop playing after the 1996 Olympics. I am 29 and need to plan for my future. I can't travel the world making $208.33 a month, what our association pays us (and what we get taxed on, along with the amount valued for our health insurance).

"The United States [field hockey team] struggles because the best players in the world are 28 to 32, and we can't keep players that long," said Fillat. "With Home Depot, playing field hockey is my job."

Home Depot, the home improvement chain, made a commitment to support Olympic athletes by giving them time off with pay and benefits to get the training and playing time they need. The company supports more than 100 Olympic athletes in this country, Canada, and Puerto Rico, more than all other companies combined. And many of these athletes are women. They get full-time pay and benefits, as well as training for a professional career, with a flexible 20-hour work week to accommodate their schedules.

Even with this support it is not easy for women to pursue athletic careers without being driven and dedicated. Fillat said she moved in with her mom at one point to save money.

Katie Kauffman, who works in the paint department at Home Depot, said the Olympic stipend for meals and lodging while the team is on the road never covers what they require. "When we go to dinner we get an allotment of money to spend; however, some days it barely gets you an entrée. As athletes, we like to eat. We are also limited to one drink. And then we are told to drink lots of fluids. So that leaves us with buying food when we go out to eat as a team." Kauffman said expenses include athletic shoes, gym fees, some travel, training clothes, laundry, and of course free-time activities. She's been on the national team since 1993, practices three weeks of every month, and trains eight to ten hours a day while on the road (two to three hours a day at home). She could not do it without her job at Home Depot.

THE NEW LOCKER ROOM

In the 1970s, when the first women sportswriters entered men's locker rooms after a game, the men were outraged. Not only did they resent having to stop walking around naked—although many did not stop—they believed their locker room was sacred.

Many women in management jobs say it is important to get into that locker room, at least the "virtual" locker room, by participating in sports outings, joining the company softball team, and getting company tickets to sporting events. Some believe this is the inside track and that important business decisions are made in the "locker room"; thus, the locker room is the way to the boardroom.

Now that more women are playing team sports and understanding how the game translates into the work world, perhaps the locker room will change. Whether or not we invade the men's locker room—literally or figuratively—may not even matter. We'll have a locker room of our own.

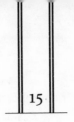

15

CELEBRATING A NEW COMMUNITY

~

*"It's like a second family. Female sports are different. You do a lot
better when you care about each other. We are nurturing people, caring
people. I'm glad to have my friends out there. It goes a little bit deeper
than just sports. We all want to see each other happy."*

—KRISTINE LILLY, USA SOCCER, TO GEORGE VECSEY,
NEW YORK TIMES REPORTER, JUNE 13, 1999

THE WOMEN WARM UP, taking shots in a junior high school gym
in Brooklyn. Only one player is sitting on the floor, legs splayed
out, doing stretches. She wears long shorts and a jersey with the
sleeves cut off. Most of the others wear long sweatpants, and few do
any warm-ups other than shooting.

These women range in age from the late 20s to late 40s. They play
a high school team because this gives the high school players more
of a challenge. The high school team's coach is a man in a sleeveless
T-shirt, knee-length cutoff sweatpants, and a bandanna tied around
his head Jerry Garcia style. For some reason, this man is occasionally allowed to play in the game.

As the warm-up shooting continues, one of the players runs
across the court and asks, "Is this the senior citizen's team?" The others hoot with laughter.

During the game, a player (number 3, the one who had done the stretches) says, "I feel like a kid." One of her friends shouts back, "You act like a kid." This player is an amazing jumper and has been grabbing most of the rebounds.

There is much joy in the air. It is palpable. Number 3's daughter and her daughter's friend are in the stands.

A gray-haired woman receives cheers from her children and husband. "Go, Mom." "Yeah, Mom." "Good job, Karen," her husband shouts.

Melissa misses a pass because she isn't quick enough and gets hit with the ball. "You OK, Melissa?" someone shouts. "Oh, shut up," she says, embarrassed at the fumble.

Throughout, there is laughter, cheering, and clapping for both teams and for all good tries. The only way you know the clapping is for a score is that the volume increases a great deal.

The smile never leaves Zan Taylor's face while she is on the court.

THE FANS LOVE US

Camaraderie and celebrating a shared experience are a big part of enjoying sports. After a good game, feeling mellow and exhausted, you can relax at your favorite café or bar and rehash the fun of the game—the great plays, the near misses. You don't get that by working out alone in a gym.

This sense of community and belonging carries over into the sports arenas where women play. Women's games are promoted as family events, where there is a sense of celebration rather than angry confrontation with players and coaches and refs yelling at each other. Ice-cream lines are longer than the beer lines.

Elena Gervino, a Hartford, Connecticut, lawyer holding a teddy bear for her four-year-old daughter Kayla at a University of Connecticut women's basketball game, told a *New York Times* reporter, "The men's games are too stressful. The fans yell at the coaches, yell at the players, yell at the officials. I guess the stakes are too high. This is a lovefest: We love the players, we love the coaches, we love UConn."

Many sports fans are losing respect for men's professional sports teams because of the abuses of power, the outrageous salary demands, the egos, the fighting, the failure to be positive role models. The men's fans, too, leave much to be desired. Some stadiums now have a special police force to monitor the behavior of spectators who fight, throw trash on the field, and pour beer on the heads of those in front of them.

The women's teams encourage the emotional attachment between the players and fans. In the official team guides, the men's biographies stick to birthdate and college major, while the women's include hobbies (running, shopping, and watching "Jeopardy"), favorite food (frozen yogurt with chocolate sprinkles), and pregame routine (curl my hair).

And this new community is global. The Louisiana Tigerettes Hi-Tops went to the Nike World Masters games to play some full-court basketball in the summer of 1998. Once they arrived in Portland, Oregon, they played against teams from Argentina, Russia, and Canada.

"The thrill was something I will be eternally grateful for," Mavis Albin said. "The language was a hindrance, but somehow we were able to communicate in getting our message understood. Some of the Russian ladies did not know how to get to their hotel. We had a rental car that should have carried three people, but we wedged five women in and transported them to their room.

"We met an FBI agent from our area, who made us feel very secure as he assured us he would look out for us should any violence erupt. He was told it was my birthday. My teammate's birthday was the next day. He ordered a cake shaped like a basketball one night, and we walked out to a large crowd, and they began to sing 'Happy Birthday' to Nikki and me in different languages. This was such a pleasant surprise. Tears flowed down my face when I looked at all the people with the big smiles on their faces singing. Even though we could not understand them, their smiles and gentle gestures said it all. For instance, one lady from Australia dug in her satchel and gave me the game shirt she had played in. We were given phone numbers, addresses, and mementos."

BONDING: IT'S JUST TOO COOL

"Bonding is an exciting thing for them," Stefanie Pemper said about the women who come to the Never Too Late clinics in Boston and New York. "Getting away for a weekend to play basketball is just too cool." It's a new form of fitness, too. Pemper believes this is one of the reasons so many women like the Never Too Late camps. Pemper, women's varsity basketball coach at Bowdoin College, also coaches at the Never Too Late weekend clinics.

"Some [women] are starving for a little instruction and think that if someone teaches them, they will improve. Or some find it a new love, or get back to it."

Never Too Late clinics and weekend camps were organized in Boston and New York and have begun to appear in other cities as well. Players get repetitive drills work on ball handling, passing, shooting, shot fakes, post play, fastbreak situations, defensive team play, and competitive games.

Leslie Davis, coach of the renowned Lady Falcons of Cambridge Rindge and Latin School, also coaches some of the Never Too Late weekend camps. She wished she could transfer the enthusiasm of the camp players to her own high school basketball team.

Allison Lee, 31, a high school teacher, signed up for Never Too Late after she got so inspired by attending a WNBA Liberty game at Madison Square Garden. She went right out looking for a game of her own. She had never played sports in her life, so she began playing with 12-year-olds in the park. Someone told her about the Never Too Late clinics, and she signed up for one in Brooklyn. "You run drills with 10 or 20 people, practice with the coach," Lee said. She also went to their summer camp. Now she plays with a pick-up group in Hoboken, New Jersey, near where she lives. The players are all ages (22 to 40), races, and professions, and they play at the local Y. Lee is trying to keep the group together and is working toward getting the team into a league of some kind.

"Basketball definitely spurs physical health," she said. "I joined a gym to get in shape for basketball." Her prebasketball fitness agenda was "heavy lifting" as part of her job as a waitress for years.

"I just want to play basketball once or twice a week for the rest of my life," said Lee.

CONNECTION AND HARMONY

"We all developed as women and athletes together," Narci Culpepper Norgaard, 31, a police officer of Bend, Oregon, said. She is one of a group of "has beens" from a 1988 college championship volleyball team, who still get together and play for fun. "We're still involved in each other's lives." Culpepper Norgaard and the others played with the Portland State Vikings.

"You can still see bits of everyone in each one of us. Our personalities always take up right where we left off the last time we were together. Truly an unusual, wonderful experience over the years, the sport enables us to create some great memories and lifetime goals. Our drive to be champions has given us the dedication to remain friends and the loyalty to that commitment."

Patty Jayne said, "I believe athletics in its purest form is a work of art. Take away the spectators, money, egos and you have uninhibited play which allows me to creatively express myself—my body, mind, and soul uniting to push and test my limits, as well as work together with those around me."

Jayne enjoys the sense of connectedness and harmony "not only within myself but with my teammates when this actually happens. Barriers are taken down and there is a feeling of power, not in a destructive or controlling sense, but an awesome achieving state; more can be accomplished together than we ever could apart. These are the things that drive me to keep at it, and that I strive to ultimately teach to those I coach. It takes great discipline however, especially on a team, so it can be difficult to achieve."

"I felt like I belonged to a group for the first time in my life," said Jen Stitzell of the Chicago Ice, who began playing hockey in college. "Hockey has only changed me for the better. It brought me out of my shell in college. As a freshman I hardly did anything but attend class and study. After I started playing, I had my core group of friends to hang out with all the time. We went to bars and movies and did typical college stuff."

A PLACE TO FEEL SUPPORTED AND SUPPORTIVE

"I love playing with this team," said Elizabeth McCarthy about her basketball teammates in the New York Urban Professionals League. "Five of the nine players have all played together for a couple of years; all share similar values and interests in life, which I think affects the way we play, and really enjoy each other's company as well as helping each other succeed. We have struggled as a team, celebrated as a team, and formed really close friendships. There was some tension last season when we had some new members with decidedly different styles and temperaments, and we had to work through some tough issues to get to a place where we are again a cohesive unit. I wouldn't bother if this were just about a game."

McCarthy got involved when a colleague at work invited her to play. "I had been training for a triathlon, so was in pretty good shape, but missed the camaraderie and sheer fun of playing basketball. I had just finished graduate school and was often struck by the fact that the guys all played sports together as a way to bond and release tension (after exams, for study breaks, etc.) while the women went for coffee or shopping. It was really disturbing to me that I had gotten away from team sports, which were once such a big part of my life.

"The team gives me a place where I feel supported and supportive," said McCarthy, "where my position and title don't matter, and where I become completely engrossed in the task at hand, not thinking about anything else that is going on in my life. I think about the games ahead of time and have trouble winding down after them. It reminds me of the way I felt about my high school team. The rest of the day I was focused on school (now work) and my own personal goals, but once I was on the court, I became one integral part of this vibrant, connected unit.

"If I miss a practice I feel guilty, because I am the one who pushes people to show up," McCarthy said, "and I am the one who gets annoyed when other people don't show. I don't miss very many games, but if I do I feel a bit left out, and a bit like I let my team down, especially if it turns out there was someone really tall for me to guard and I wasn't there.

"I have been to the weddings, birthdays, and going-away parties of many teammates over the years," McCarthy said, "plus the more informal times getting a beer after the game, or having a preseason (or postseason) dinner. I have had the team out to my beach house and have been to many of their homes.

"The high I get from playing—the adrenaline flow—is different than that which I get from running or working out. Basketball is fun, competitive, and can be rough. It allows me to have an outlet for stress, ensures that I take time away from work to exercise, socialize, and stop thinking, and is one of the only chances I get as a grown woman to care nothing about the way I look, speak, or present myself. I think it is also a place to try new things with very little at risk, to set goals, and to really test physical capabilities."

IT'S WHERE WE ARE

Cindy Powell was flabbergasted by the outpouring of support she got from her teammates at Alexandria Community Rowing when she was hospitalized after waking up in the middle of the night with a fluke nosebleed.

"It was bizarre and had no apparent reason, but I lost 25 percent of my blood through my nose." Hospitalized for several days, she said, "I was floored by the support I got from the others. They sent me flowers as a group. They visited me at the hospital and later at home—where I found a card waiting. I got E-mails from people, just notes. I didn't think they knew me or missed me.

"My dad flew up. He's a doctor and wanted to be sure my doctors were taking good care of me. And he was really impressed with all the support from the rowers, so he told the doctors, 'My daughter's an athlete, a competitive rower.'

" 'I am?' was all I could say. I still can't believe it."

Believe it! It's where we are now, finally.

RESOURCES

THERE ARE WOMEN'S TEAMS all over the country, and many of them have their own websites. Some you can find through links from the major sports sites, but others take more searching. The following list of organizations and women's sports leagues and teams can help you get started.

Included in this directory are organizations that provide information about training and avoiding injury, as well as where to find assistance in fighting gender discrimination in sports programs.

BASEBALL

Women's National Adult Baseball Association (WNABA)
5173 Waring Road, Suite 750
San Diego, CA 92120

800-949-6222 or 619-265-7048
Fax: 619-229-0786
E-mail: WNABA@aol.com

Formed in 1994, this organization was inspired by the movie *A League of Their Own*. It's the only national organized league for women's baseball, although smaller local leagues are scattered around the country with teams in 20 cities.

BASKETBALL

Women's National Basketball Association
Website: www.WNBA.com

This website links to all the WNBA teams, has the latest news about the teams and players, and includes information about basketball camps and tryout dates.

The National Association of Midnight Basketball Leagues
1980 Mountain Boulevard, Suite 214
Oakland, CA 94611-2834
510-339-1272
Fax: 510-339-2864
E-mail: midnightbasketball@juno.com
Website: www.bayscenes.com/NP/midnightball/

This organization was set up to help young men at risk. Recently it began to include basketball for girls and young women with teams in several cities, including San Jose, California, and Cleveland, Ohio.

National Women's Basketball League
619-692-4447
Fax: 707-248-2248

E-mail: leagueoffice@nwbl

Website: www.nwbl.com

This semipro basketball league for women who are former college athletes or who have never played has teams across the United States. You may also find them through your local health club or YMCA.

Never Too Late

P.O. Box 235

West Medford, MA 02156

781-488-3333

888-NTL-HOOPS

E-mail: hoops@nevertoolate.com

Website: www.nevertoolate.com

This organization operates weekend basketball camps and week-night clinics for women and men in various cities. They began in Boston and New York, and now operate camps in Santa Barbara, California; Lakeside, Michigan; and Sheffield, Massachusetts.

Nancy Lieberman-Cline Basketball Camp

P.O. Box 79054

Dallas, TX 75379-5054

Website: www.girlsbasketballcamps.com/Nancy

Women's Basketball Fantasy Camp

P.O. Box 2864

Gilbert, AZ 85299-2864

602-539-6125

Website: www.wmgaz.com

This camp is operated by WMG Comprehensive Sports Management.

Amateur Athletic Union (AAU)
407-934-7200
Website: www.aaugirlsbasketball.org

Look on the website for a link to *Gball*, the girls basketball magazine, or find it at gballmag.com.

FIELD HOCKEY

United States Field Hockey
One Olympic Plaza
Colorado Springs, CO 80909-5773
719-578-4567
E-mail: usfha@usfieldhockey.com
Website: www.usfieldhockey.com

The website of the national team has links to other field hockey organizations.

FOOTBALL

International Women's Flag Football Association
1107 Key Plaza, Suite 233
Key West, FL 33040-4077
305-293-9315 or 888-GO-IWFFA
Website: www.iwffa.com

Women's Professional Football League
5555 West 78th Street, Suite B
Edina, MN 55439
877-922-2695 or 952-833-2029
Fax: 952-833-0916

E-mail: wwsports@visi.com

Website: www.womensprofootball.com

This fledgling league has more than a dozen teams divided up into four regional conferences in the United States. The website links to all teams. By 2002 they hope to have 11 more expansion teams. They had a 10-game inaugural season in 2000.

ICE HOCKEY

Chicago Ice

E-mail: chgoice@mcs.net

Website: www.mcs.net/~chgoice/

Connect with the members of Chicago's premier women's ice hockey organization.

USA Hockey

517-547-6565 (USA Hockey Girls/Women's Section Director)

Website: www.usahockey.com

The first step, according to USA Hockey, in joining an ice hockey team in your area is to call or visit your local rink or hockey association. If you are unable to locate a program in your area, contact one of the representatives listed on this website for assistance.

The Women's Hockey Web

Website: www.whockey.com

This website includes links to most women's hockey clubs in the United States and Canada. It also gives information on camps, tournaments, players, and college programs.

LACROSSE

Quickstix
300 Unity Lane
Annapolis, MD 21401
410-573-9772
Fax: 410-573-0052
E-mail: samara@quickstix.com
Website: www.quickstix.com

This organization helps promote women's lacrosse and assists schools and clubs in organizing teams. The website includes a comprehensive calendar of games, clinics, and news of recent events, leagues, and tournaments.

United States National Lacrosse
113 West University Parkway
Baltimore, MD 21210
410-235-6882
Fax: 410-366-6735
E-mail: info@lacrosse.org
Website: www.lacrosse.org

While this site covers men and women, there is extensive news about women's lacrosse camps, clinics, and clubs.

ROWING

Alexandria Community Rowing
P.O. Box 16431
Alexandria, VA 11302
703-660-3450
Website: www.rowalexandria.org

The website includes current races, photos of rowing teams, and links to other rowing sites.

Row as One
421 High Street
Westwood, MA 02090
781-326-4648
E-mail: rowasone@tiac.net
Website: www.tiac.net/users/rowasone

Through camps, team clinics, coaching, and program development, the Row as One Institute's goal is to develop a safe learning environment for women and girls of all abilities and backgrounds through recreational and competitive rowing.

U.S. Rowing
800-314-4ROW
E-mail: row2k@row2k.com
Website: www.row2k.com

The official site for the United States National Rowing Team includes links to other women's rowing sites.

SAILING

National Women's Sailing Association (NWSA)
16731 McGregor Boulevard
Fort Myers, FL 33908
800-566-NWSA or 941-454-0035
Fax: 941-454-5859
E-mail: wsf@womensailing.org
Website: www.sailnet.com/nwsa

The National Women's Sailing Association is a project of the Women's Sailing Foundation, Inc., a nonprofit organization dedicated to enriching the lives of women and girls through education and access to the sport of sailing. NWSA publishes the *Take the Helm* newsletter.

U.S. Sailing
P.O. Box 1260
Portsmouth, RI 02871-0907
401-683-0800
Website: www.ussailing.org/championship/Rolex

U.S. Sailing is the national governing body of the sport of sailing.

Womanship
137 Conduit Street
Annapolis, MD 21401
800-342-9295 or 410-267-6661
E-mail: Womanship@aol.com
Website: www.womanship.com

A sailing school by and for women, Womanship schedules classes in various parts of the world and for various lengths of time. They have conducted classes in Chesapeake Bay, the Bahamas, Florida, the Great Lakes region, Southern California, New England, Long Island Sound, the British Virgin Islands, and British Columbia, among other places.

SOCCER

United States Amateur Soccer Association
Website: www.usasa.com

This website has information about how to organize and set up a soccer league in your neighborhood, where to find coaches, and how to gain community support.

Women's Soccer Foundation
P.O. Box 600404
Newton, MA 02460
617-243-9487
Fax: 617-243-0827
Website: www.womensoccer.org

This nonprofit organization is dedicated to strengthening the voice of girls and women in soccer throughout the world. They have a newsletter and links to other sites.

SOFTBALL

Amateur Softball Association of America (ASA)
Website: www.softball.org

As the national governing body of softball in the United States, the ASA regulates competition to ensure fairness and equal opportunity to the thousands of teams, umpires, and sponsors involved in the sport.

Women's Professional Softball League
Website: www.prosoftball.com

The website includes news of tryouts and games, merchandise, and links to the teams.

USA Softball
Website: www.usasoftball.com

Website of the national softball team, this site carries news and try-out information.

VOLLEYBALL

United States Professional Volleyball League (USPV)
1555 Mittel Boulevard, Suite J
Wood Dale, IL 60191
630-787-9950
Fax: 630-787-9958
E-mail: contact@uspv.com
Website: www.uspv.com

This is the first professional volleyball league in the United States that began with all women's teams. The website includes team profiles, news of "Dream Team" tournaments, and plans for their 2002 launch as a competitive league. There are links to other volleyball sites as well as other women's sports sites.

USA Volleyball
Website: www.usavolleyball.org

The USA volleyball website offers information on the national volleyball teams as well as youth and beach volleyball teams.

National Senior Games Association
3032 Old Forge Drive
Baton Rouge, LA 70808
Website: www.nsga.com

This organization promotes sports among people over 50 and sponsors tournaments in various age groups. The website has links to state senior games organizations and news of Olympic games.

WomenSport International (WSI)
P.O. Box 743
Vashon, WA 98070
Website: www.de.psu.edu/wsi/

WomenSport International was formed to meet the challenge of ensuring that sport and physical activity receive the attention and priority they deserve in the lives of girls and women. WSI is both an issues- and action-based organization. Members represent 30 countries and a broad range of expertise and interest in the areas of sports science, medicine, health and fitness, nutrition, coaching, administration, and education.

Women's Sports Foundation (WSF)
Eisenhower Park
East Meadow, NY 11554
800-277-3988
Website: www.WomensSportsFoundation.org

Founded in 1974 by Billie Jean King, the Women's Sports Foundation is a charitable educational organization dedicated to increasing the participation of girls and women in sports and fitness and creating an educated public that supports gender equity in sport. The foundation's education, participation, advocacy, research, and leadership programs are made possible by individual and corporate contributions.

Women in Sports Careers Foundation
714-848-1201
Fax: 714-848-5111
E-mail: wiscfoundation@aol.com
Website: www.wiscfoundation.org

The mission of the Women in Sports Careers Foundation is to provide women and girls with professional guidance, education, and support to pursue sports-related careers. The website includes a chat room and Women's Sports Wire for the latest news.

The Melpomene Institute
1010 University Avenue
St. Paul, MN 55104
651-642-1951
Fax: 651-642-1871
E-mail: health@melpomene.org
Website: www.melpomene.org

The Melpomene Institute is dedicated to the study and research of women and physical activity. A variety of resources are available through the website, such as tips for parents who want to encourage their daughters and a questionnaire to help parents and students assess the athletic equality in their schools.

Tucker Center for Research on Girls and Women in Sport (CRGWS)
University of Minnesota
203 Cooke Hall
1900 University Avenue, SE
612-625-7327
Fax: 612-626-7700
E-mail: crgws@tc.umn.edu
Website: www.kls.coled.umn.edu/crgws/

CRGWS is an interdisciplinary research center dedicated to examining how sport and physical activity impact the lives of young girls and women. Community outreach and mentoring students is another goal of the organization. The website is a source of current research, news, and an on-line newsletter.

SPORTS MEDICINE AND HEALTH

Cincinnati Sports Medicine and Orthopaedic Center
513-559-2810
Website: www.deaconess-healthcare.com/services/sportsmed.html

The website has information on exercises and training for soccer and other team sports, including ways to reduce head and neck injuries and knee injuries. A videotape can be ordered by calling 513-346-7290, ext. 3707.

Women's Sports Medicine Center
Hospital for Special Surgery
535 East 70th Street
New York, NY 10021
212-606-1345
Website: www.hss.edu/htdoc/womensport

The website provides advice for athletes about conditioning and avoiding injury and tips on first aid, how to avoid getting over-heated, and the best kinds of clothing for extreme weather conditions.

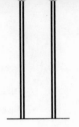

INDEX

ABOUT THE AUTHOR

MARIAN BETANCOURT has written more than a dozen books and hundreds of magazine and newspaper articles, many about issues important to women. Her 1997 book, *What to Do When Love Turns Violent: A Resource for Women in Abusive Relationships*, was praised in the *New York Times* and on "Oprah." She lives in New York and is a rabid fan of the New York Liberty, as well as being a member of the Women's Sports Foundation and the National Women's Sailing Association.